I0473624

MICHELANGELO MEETS SINAN

Representations of the Divine, Salvation and Paradise in Renaissance Art

METIN MUSTAFA

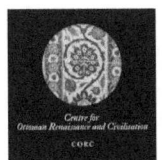

Centre for Ottoman Renaissance and Civilisation
Sydney
©2021

Copyright ©2021 by Centre for Ottoman Renaissance and Civilisation

All rights reserved. No part of this book may be reproduced or transmitted in any form or by any means, electronic or mechanical, including photocopying, recording or by any information storage and retrieval system without permission in writing from the Publisher and Author.

Published by Centre for Ottoman Renaissance and Civilisation

Email: info@ottomanrenaisance.org

Website: ottomanrenaissance.org

ISBN: 978-0-646-83153-4

Cover Design: Centre for Ottoman Renaissance and Civilisation

The true work of art is but a shadow of the divine perfection. Michelangelo

I acquired a sought-after bit of wisdom from the crenellation of great ancient remains and a provision of knowledge from every ruined monument. Sinan

Other books by the author:

History of Ottoman Renaissance Art:
From Mehmed I to Selim II. Revised Edition.

The Ottoman Renaissance:
A Reconsideration of Early Modern Ottoman Art, 1413-1575

Tragedy of Sultan Süleyman (a play)

CONTENTS

INTRODUCTION

T his discussion seeks to explore the analogies of early modern Ottoman art aesthetics with the aesthetics of Renaissance art of Italy. This book aims to re-orient the narrative of Sinan's use of the fine art of Iznik *çini* (tiles) within the context of the Renaissance humanist paradigm. The study compares the fine art of Iznik *çini* of the Mosque of Rustem Pasha (1560-61) by the Ottoman imperial architect and artist Sinan, with the monumental *buon' fresco* of one of the giants of the Renaissance—Michelangelo's *Last Judgement* in the Sistine Chapel in the Vatican (1541). The alternative reading of these two works, as undertaken in this study, looks beyond the grand-scale production of the two works in order to examine the allegorical message they convey. Such a comparison underpins the Mediterranean *zeitgeist* exemplified by the early modern art of Italy and Ottoman Istanbul in the sixteenth century. Inspired by their respective religious and intellectual traditions, the works of Michelangelo and Sinan converge thematically. Close analysis of the two works from anagogical and eschatological paradigms based on the religious themes alluded to in the New Testament and the Qur'an respectively: 'Salvation', 'Act of Judgement', 'Self-reflection' and 'Predestination' including the *Isra* and *Mi'raj* narratives of Prophet Muhammad influencing Dante's (d. 1321) *Divine Comedy*, establish the meeting point between Michelangelo and Sinan. Furthermore, applying the Sufi humanist, Ibn Arabi's (1165-1240) theophanic (visible manifestations of God to humankind) experience of the Divine, and the Jungian theory of religious symbolisms providing a deeper sense of meaning to one's existence, the book establishes a link between the art of Michelangelo and Sinan. From these perspectives the pan-European notion of the Renaissance begins to dissipate and instead offers a more inclusive understanding of the period in discussion. Therefore, the underpinning of this argument promotes the broadening of our understanding of the shared heritage in the Mediterranean during the sixteenth century (*Figures 1, 2*).

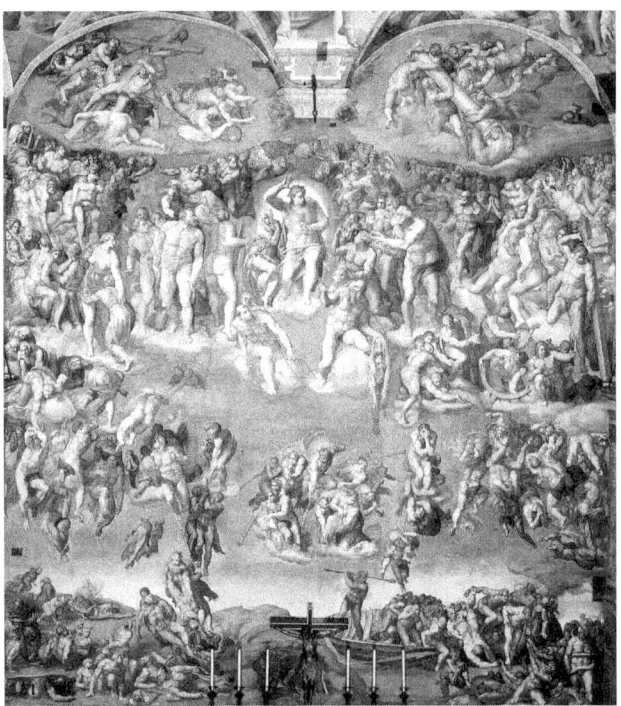

Figure 1. Photograph of 'The Last Judgement' of Michelangelo, Sistine Chapel, Vatican Museum. Photograph reproduction.

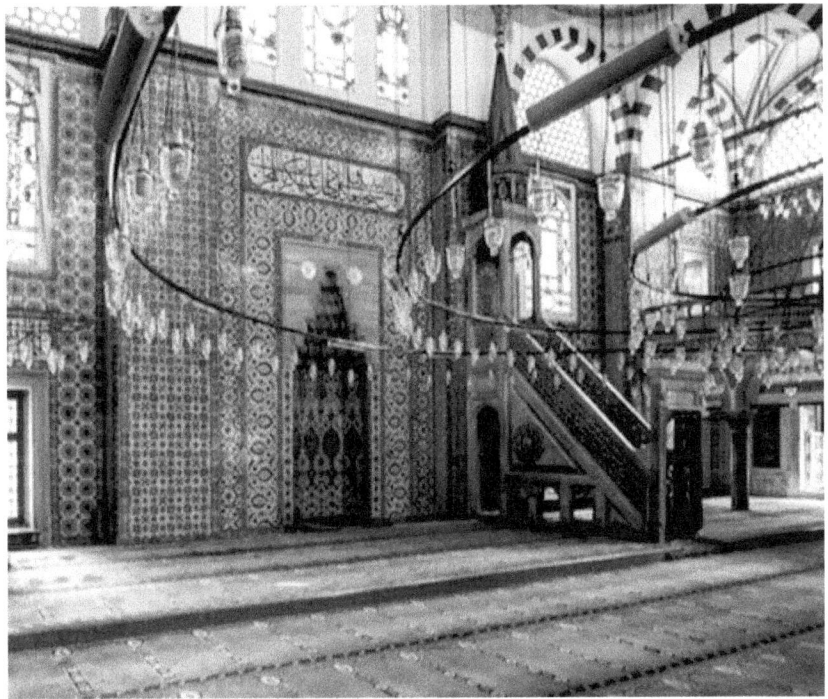

Figure 2. View of the qibla wall, the mihrab and mimbar from the balcony of the Rustem Pasha Mosque, Istanbul, c.1560-61. Photograph by Metin Mustafa, December 13, 2015.

Prominent art historian Gülru Necipoğlu, calls for a "fresh narrative" to "negotiate the alterity" of early modern Ottoman art.[1] Necipoğlu invites scholars to explore its "analogies with the Renaissance in Italy."[2] The revisionist perspective explored in this work is a response to that call. The two artworks, Michelangelo's fresco *Last Judgement* (1536-41) and Sinan's use of the Iznik *çini* in the interior decoration of Mosque Rustem Pasha (1560-61) respectively, physically manifest reflective intentions to inspire spiritual and inward contemplation, and to establish a connection between the individual and the Divine, seeking salvation and paradise in the afterlife. In 1964, Carl G. Jung wrote:

With the drawing of the Renaissance, a revolutionary change began to occur in man's conception of the world. The "upward" movement (which reached its climax in the late Middle Ages) went into reverse; man turned back to the earth. He rediscovered the beauties of nature and the body, made the first circumnavigation of the globe, and proved the world to be a sphere. The laws of mechanics and causality became the foundations of science. The world of religious feeling, of the irrational, and of mysticism, which had played so great a part in medieval times, was more and more submerged by the triumphs of logical thought.[3]

However, the Renaissance did not completely make a break from the religious ideas and themes of the Middle Ages as claimed by Jung. The triumph of logical thought took some time to come to fruition, for the sixteenth century man, despite embracing the visible world, was still content in accepting the eternal life to come in the Hereafter. As Jung attests, "In spite of the far-reaching changes in art, philosophy, and science brought about by the Renaissance, the central symbol of Christianity remained unchanged. Christ was still represented on the Latin cross, as he is today."[4] The holiest place in Christendom perhaps outside Jerusalem is St Peter's in Rome for in the history of symbolism its altar stands in the centre of the basilica as its central focus, symbol of Christ offering the hope of salvation for humanity. Similarly, the sacred focal point for Islam since its inception in the seventh century remained the Ka'ba in Mecca symbolically represented by the *mihrab* in mosque interior decorative aesthetics. Throughout the centuries Muslim architects engaged in embellishing one of the most significant features of mosque architectural elements – the *mihrab*. Situated in the centre of the *qibla* wall of the mosque interior the *mihrab* has become the symbol of the Ka'ba. The Ka'ba, as the central focus of all Muslims during their five daily prayers, serves as the ethereal home for the believers – the symbolic House of God on earth and a sacred place reflecting the Hereafter.[5] For Muslims, the holy temple at Mecca is a replica of *Al-bayt al-ma'mūr* (The Inhabited House) in the Seventh

Heaven.[6] The Inhabited House (*Al-bayt al-ma'mūr*) according to Imam Bukhari (810-870) is a house, which is located in the Seventh Heaven.[7] The Qur'an refers to it as the "Much-Frequented House" (52:4). It is directly above the Ka'ba. According Abu Sa'id al-Khudri (612-693), one of the companions of the Prophet, seventy thousand angels perform the *tawaf* (circumambulation) of this house like the pilgrims and worshippers do around the Ka'ba during Hajj and Umrah rituals.[8] Therefore, it can be argued that standing in front of the *mihrab* the worshipper is acting like the angelic figures praising the Lord. Its religious symbolism in mosque architecture is therefore highly significant, one that continued to evolve aesthetically for centuries serving a prominent role in the sacred space.

The architectural feature of the *mihrab* became more and more artistically elaborate and grand in design in imperial mosques of the Ottoman Empire during the sixteenth century occupying the most pivotal point in mosque interior design, further accentuating its symbolic significance as a reminder of the Hereafter and attaining salvation. This distinctively Islamic architectural feature was decorated not only with Qur'anic calligraphy but more specifically abstract floral naturalism symbolising the paradise promised in the Qur'an.

Imbued in the two diametrically contrasting works of Michelangelo and Sinan respectively lay ecclesiastical mysticism. Nineteenth century painter of German expressionism, Franz Marc (1880-1916), describing the objective of abstract artists in the following words also resonate with the two Renaissance contemporaries, Michelangelo and Sinan:

> [...] it must be realized that what these artists were concerned with was something greater than a problem of form and the distinction between "concrete" and "abstract", figurative and non-figurative. Their goal was the center of life and things, their changeless background, and an inward certitude. Art had become mysticism.[9]

Religious mysticism intertwined with art played a significant role in the production of artworks during the Renaissance. Just as the resurrection of the souls from their graves and the Second Coming of Christ dominates Michelangelo's *Last Judgement* fresco, so too, in Sinan's works, Prophet Muhammad's Night Journey (*Isra*) and Ascension to the Seven Heavens (*Mir'aj*) provided artistic inspiration needed to create his interior decorative aesthetics in the Rustem Pasha Mosque. According to architectural historian, Phoebe Crisman, works created allow for "paying attention, and reflective states that are considered to contribute more to psychological, intellectual, and spiritual development, rather than the kind of calming contemplation which might be seeking to eliminate thought."[10] This meditative and transcendental notion is consistent with Sufi mysticism, with which Sinan was closely associated.[11] Inspired by his Islamic faith, the Qur'anic representations of the world to come and that of the ascension of Prophet Muhammad during his *mi'raj*, whereby the Prophet was shown Paradise and Hell, and finally attaining Union with God (*Ittihad*), Sinan set to transform early modern Ottoman art aesthetics to reflect this esoteric experience. Similarly, Michelangelo inspired by Dante's (d. 1321) imaginative vision of the afterlife in the *Divine Comedy*, set out to reflect the world to come and the saving of the souls after death by the Second Coming of Christ. Through a theophanic experience, this discussion seeks to elucidate the spiritual and transcendental contemplation of Michelangelo's *Last Judgement* and Sinan's use of Iznik *çini* in the Mosque of Rustem Pasha. Furthermore, the ostensible relationship between the tiles of the Rustem Pasha Mosque and Michelangelo's fresco is the result of the shared sixteenth century Mediterranean *zeitgeist* (spirit of the age) between Italy and Ottoman Istanbul during the Renaissance.

Additionally, at a figurative level—Michelangelo's *Last Judgement* focuses on the personal and spiritual struggle of the artist himself; intertwined with the intense political and social chaos of Protestantism, which was contemporaneous with the work's creation. Likewise, it explores the Catholic Church's response to this through the Counter-Reformation, which gave the popes of the day universal justification for such a cause. While religious and political tensions are not evident in Sinan's Mosque of Rustem Pasha, Sinan's purpose for creating the work is similar to that of his Renaissance counterpart, that is, as a celebration. The mosque serves as reverence to the Grand Vizier's patronage and the Ottoman court's global perception of itself as having created an earthly paradise. Whilst the theological differences between Christianity and Islam allow the two art forms to demonstrate a divergent stylistic path along their respective traditions, in an eschatological sense they are united by their aesthetic and thematic purpose. Through the High Renaissance mannerist style, present in both Michelangelo's reliance on abstraction and Sinan's floral naturalism, the two art forms converge to unite the New Testament and Qur'anic narratives through a didactic argument. This didactic nature of the two works allows for individual self-examination.

A comparison of this nature is unique, as scholars have not considered it before—likely due to what they perceived to be great dissimilarities between the art forms. Thus, such a comparative analysis is timely and significant by demonstrating the shared artistic heritage of the Mediterranean Renaissance. Underlying all the achievements of early modern civilisations, according to Ayesha Ramachandran,

> [There] is a need to synthesize new global experiences into a structure that would bind individual fragments into a collective unity. To comprehend the world thus required deft oscillation between local details and global frameworks and a reconfiguration of the particular against the universal.[12]

Giving voice to the two Renaissance contemporaries allows for deeper insights into the mindsets of Michelangelo and Sinan that underscores a more culturally inclusive interpretation of the Mediterranean *zeitgeist* that exemplified the sixteenth century. By comparing the two artworks there is the realisation that according to Jung, "It is the role of religious symbols to give meaning to the life of man ... [and] a sense of a wider meaning to one's existence."[13]

Michelangelo and Sinan: In their own words

One of the most influential forces for Michelangelo and Sinan is their religious belief and their relationship with God. Religion has contributed to the formation of inspiration for both artists. George Raymond in his book, *Art in Theory* states:

> The products of art are to be ascribed to what is termed inspiration. When we have traced them to this overflow at the very springs of mental vitality, no one who thinks can fail to feel that, if human life anywhere can come into contact with the divine life, it must be here.[14]

Both artists believed that their art was a direct reflection of God, and that they could come to know God better through their art. This feeling of connection between God and the creation of art can be seen very clearly through Michelangelo's own poetry and Sinan's autobiographies. In his poetry, Michelangelo writes:

> From ink, from pen in hand we see outflow / the several styles: high, low, and in-between; / so out of stone come noble forms or mean, / depending on how imaginative the art. / And, my dear Lord, it's like that with your heart: / Humility's there in equal parts with pride. // I only see what's most like me inside / that heart of yours. As smile or grimace shows. / One who's flung seed of grief, pain, woe abroad / (rain falls, itself as pure, but changes straight in seedbeds to rank earths variety), / He'll reap the same, by pain and sorrow gnawed. // Who eyes great beauty through a grief as great sees only his suffering soul, racked with anxiety.[15]

This poem reflects the connection of Michelangelo's art with his God. References to his talent coming from God and forming art "out of stone come from noble forms" acknowledge the divine inspiration of his artwork. Furthermore, although he can see great beauty in the world through this grief, he can only see his own "suffering soul" for which he holds God responsible.

Similarly, Sinan in his autobiographies acknowledge the greatness of God and the gifts He bestowed on him to create his works of art. In his architectural treatise Sinan praises God:

> Let there be unsurpassed praise and grateful acclaim for that self-sufficient Sovereign who brought humankind into the realm of existence and honoured and exalted it above all creation ... Praise and thanks and unsurpassed glory upon the matchless Creator ... Who, in accord with the noble verse in the Qur'an, "And [have We not] built for you the seven firmaments?," without architect or builder and without column or pier made apparent and manifest above the earth's pure face the green vault and spreading canopy of the heavens.[16]

After his exaltation of God and acknowledging the greatness of the Divine Architect Sinan's scribe Sa'i praises the architect's gifts:

> If there were no architect to build the world, with stone alone, no wall could be made. Above all, a wise architect such as this, a master engineer, pious and without defect: Sinan of Kayseri is his celebrated name.[17]

Acknowledging the greatness of Sinan, the treatise, like Michelangelo's expression of his personal sorrow and grief in his poem above, admits that "Sinan of Kayseri, too [like the architects of the Hagia Sophia] has suffered many troubles during the completion of each [of his] buildings, all of which, no doubt with the help of God, came into existence ..."[18]

The religious underpinnings exemplified in the works of Michelangelo and Sinan are reflective of the spirit of the age in the Mediterranean basin during the Renaissance. Such a global framework allows room for Ottoman art, particularly Sinan's, to be integrated into the Renaissance discourse. Therefore, the anagogical and eschatological analysis of the aesthetics of Michelangelo's *Last Judgement* and the Iznik *çini* of Sinan's Mosque of Rustem Pasha, underpin the shared cultural heritage of these Renaissance masterpieces. Before exploring the anagogical and eschatological readings of the two artworks, it is pertinent to gain contextual understanding of the Renaissance and the Mediterranean *zeitgeist* exemplified by the two contemporaries of the age—Michelangelo and Sinan.

PART I

CHAPTER 1

THE RENAISSANCE AND THE MEDITERRANEAN ZEITGEIST

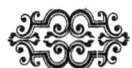

The critique of Eurocentrism has generated a new interest in exploring the extensive global interaction of Italian visual culture with the Islamic East and the New World in the early modern period. However, the current trend to reframe the Italian Renaissance in a more multicultural paradigm, which acknowledges its hybridity and heterogeneity, has had little impact in the conceptual framing of Ottoman [visual culture].[1]

The challenge for art historians begins with the term 'Renaissance' and its ever-changing interpretation through the centuries to suit the historical context of the time. The aim of this chapter is to briefly explore the dominant Vasarian understanding of the Renaissance and its historiographical, indeed historical, impact from the sixteenth to the twenty-first century. By the nineteenth century, the Vasarian context was lost on the new interpreters of Renaissance. Men like Jacob Burckhardt and Jules Michelet took from Vasari's work certain absolute truths of the idea that the Renaissance witnessed the birth of the modern individual. As authoritative scholars in their own right, Burckhardt and Michelet influenced generations, with the Renaissance coming to symbolise the beginning of European modernity. Such modernist perspectives on the Renaissance are now interpreted in the context of nineteenth-century nationalism and colonialism as offering models of civilisation with concomitant ideas of cultural superiority and the right to rule and define the 'Other' through their eyes. The periods of exploration, empire building and European colonisation contributed to the spread of these European ideals. With twentieth-century wars and associated decolonisation, the bubble of civilisation burst and the narrative of Vasari's Renaissance was called into question. Indeed, with the hindsight of the twenty-first century, reframing the definition of Renaissance is a high priority not only for Western scholars but also for non-European scholars, especially for cultures in the Mediterranean basin, which share a historical legacy with their European counterparts.

Directly engaging with this new historiographical trend, this discussion reshapes the notion of the Renaissance by uniquely looking at Ottoman, rather than Vasarian, understandings of rebirth, specifically through the contemporary work of Mimar Sinan. This chapter, therefore, establishes a more meaningful and specifically Ottoman definition that permits a reading of Ottoman artistic production both within its own context and within a more global one. Beginning with the Vasarian perception of the Renaissance, followed by nineteenth to twenty-first century developments in Renaissance historiography, then continuing with the Ottoman view of the same, the chapter not only reviews the main body of literature in the field but sets up the theoretical foundation for the book as a whole.

The Vasarian paradigm

The Renaissance is traditionally associated with the revival of classical Greek and Roman literature, philosophy, and art and the aesthetic and intellectual innovations they inspired. The Renaissance is also typically associated with the Florentines of the late fourteenth to mid-sixteenth centuries. Giorgio Vasari's *The Lives of the Painters, Sculptors and Architects*, published in 1550 and again in 1565, was the most authoritative written articulation of Renaissance. [2] The Vasarian *rinascita* saw ideals of progress and perfection as its key qualities.[3] Indeed, within his Tuscan-centric vision, Vasari argued that "perfection" had been attained by Tuscan artists alone. These artists occupied a privileged position in history, appointed by God to revive and indeed surpass the arts of the ancients and to launch their contemporaries into a bright future entirely embedded in a Christian framework. Vasari's narrative exerted influence well into the twentieth century, being the most influential Renaissance text composed in the West.

In its literal translation, the verb *rinascere* means, "to be born again." In his *Lives,* Vasari uses the term specifically to characterise the stages of art development up until his own day. For Vasari, the perfection of the classical arts in his own time took centuries to attain, suggesting that it was an evolving process: " . . . the rise of the arts to perfection [the classical past], their decline [the Middle Ages] and their restoration or, to say it better, renaissance."[4] Vasari unambiguously introduces the notion of *rinascita* into the discourse of the period. For Vasari, this rebirth of the arts was a gradual process that took approximately three centuries, beginning with the works of Cimabue (1240–1302) and "improving little by little from a humble beginning, and finally . . . arriv[ing] at the height of perfection"[5] via Michelangelo (1483–1520) in Vasari's own time. This slow trajectory towards perfection evolved through distinct stages including *imitazione* (imitation) and *adeguazione* (adaptation), both of which were necessary to surpass classical models and achieve *perfezione* (perfection) in Vasari's temporal present.

Vasari's narrative is imbued with a humanist impulse typical of his day—the close imitation of the classical past and the astute adaptation of those models in the present. Emulating ancient classical authors like Aristotle and Pliny, the *Lives* is a biographical celebration that links Vasari's temporality to both past and future, yet maintains a focused relevance to his contemporary day. Such imitation of the past was part and parcel of Vasari's characterisation of the Medici rulers to whom he had dedicated his work. In part three of the text he praised their contributions to the city of Florence in a true Aristotelian manner, signifying the permanence of their magnificence: " . . . men of rare and beautiful genius, from whom the world receives such beauty, honour, convenience and benefit, deserve to live forever in the minds and memories of mankind."[6] This panegyric, delivered through congratulatory rhetoric and self-aggrandisement to promote the excellence of Florence, has at its core a desire to claim uncontested superiority.

Leonardo Bruni's *Panegyric to the City of Florence* (c. 1401) is a fine precedent to Vasari's civic self-fashioning. In humanistic style, Bruni wrote in imitation of Aelius Aristides's *Panathenicus* (*Panegyric to Athens*, 117–81). Hans Baron argues that Bruni cast his work on the classical model because it spoke directly to contemporary Florentines in the fashioning of their cultural identity. Indeed, Bruni ascribes to Florentines all the virtues associated with Aristides's Athens (well-known even in Vasari's day as the cultural capital of the Greek world) in an attempt to identify Florence as the new Athens of its time.[7]

Yet by Vasari's time the path of emulation and imitation was already well-trodden. From as early as the eleventh century onwards, Vasari informs us, artists began adapting and imitating classical remnants. For example, in the 1016 Duomo of Santa Maria Assunta in Siena, the Pisan architect Buschetto relied on " . . . endless quantity of spoils brought by sea from various distant parts, as the columns, bases, capitals, cornices and other stones . . . of all sizes, great, medium, and small . . . Buschetto displayed great judgment and skill in adapting them to their places . . . the façade . . . consisting of a great number of columns, adorning it with other carved columns and antique statues."[8] The adaptation of classical remains went hand in hand with the imitation of past precedents. By the fourteenth century Tuscan architect, Andrea Taffi, was imitating classical doors, windows, columns, arches and cornices " . . . with the same Greek manner, but indeed much more beautiful in the church of San Giovanni in their city."[9] In the Church of Santa Maria della Spina in Pisa (1323), Giovanni Pisano's works of sculpture "brought ornaments in that oratory to that perfection that is seen today."[10] For Vasari, Pisano demonstrated "grace," "style," and "excellence" of invention, which he saw as prerequisites for distinction.[11]

To surpass the greats of the antique past required skill. For Vasari, this meant the artist had to demonstrate precision, intellect, and patience.

According to Vasari, Michelangelo was one such man who "gave his attention only to the perfection of art" to attain a higher "degree of refinement," which could be only realised through devotion to "minute" and "delicate" details.[12]

Michelangelo's *David* (1501–4), clothed in God's glory, epitomises His perfection and the Christian message of man's triumph. This first revival of the ancient male nude who stands over four metres tall in monumental form depicts its subject patiently waiting for battle against the giant Goliath. As a Christian hero writ large, *David* overshadowed any extant antique sculpture of comparable character. This Renaissance representation of the figure of David is appropriated from the ancient Greek statue of a standing heroic male nude, the *Doryphorus* of Polykleitos (450–400 BCE), which is thought of as a distinctive style of antique sculpture for its solidly built, well-muscled standing warrior. The nudes of Greco-Roman art are conceived of as perfected ideals of heroic qualities, and *David* epitomised the rebirth of the "perfect" Renaissance Christian hero.

Both the *Doryphorus* and *David* statues are in the same *contrapposto* pose. The right leg carries the weight with the left leg positioned slightly behind it to suggest movement. Both have their weapon of choice on the left arm. Although the spear is no longer there, it too would have rested on Doryphorus's left shoulder. Like *Doryphorus*, the sculpture of *David* effectively conveys the feeling that David is in motion, an impression heightened by his *contrapposto* stance, the twist in his body heightening the figure's animation. In the biblical context of Michelangelo's *David*, David appears to take a moment between conscious choice and action—a man of logical thinking and reason—a Renaissance trait that characterised humanist thought of the time.[13] His facial expression looks drawn, and his neck tense and the bulging veins on his right hand reflect this. Like his classical hero counterparts, *David* stands ready to face his giant enemy Goliath, to demonstrate his heroic qualities, his "perfect" form clothed and protected by God; it is only through this perfection that he can truly defeat his adversary.

Michelangelo achieves this impression of perfection by foreshortening the body and sacrificing perfect proportions to accommodate the viewer's intended position below the sculpture, and enlarging the hands and eyes for effect. By adjusting the "perfect" Greek model for dramatic effect, Michelangelo's *David* becomes a Christian hero, for which he ultimately is more perfect than the statues of pagans celebrated since antiquity. With *David*, Michelangelo's work reflected the rebirth of the classical beauty of the human body as well as the Christian God's handiwork. In Vasari's words, *David* surpassed the ancient nude: " . . . [w]hen it was built up, and all was finished, he uncovered it, and it cannot be denied that this work has carried off the palm from all other statues, modern or ancient, Greek or Latin."[14] According to Vasari, Michelangelo's genius makes him unparalleled: " . . . no one . . . has ever equalled him in perfection of finish [and] that, wherever he turned his thought, brain, and mind, he displayed such divine power in his works, that, in giving them their perfection, no one was ever his peer in readiness, vivacity, excellence, beauty, and grace." [15] For Vasari, the perfection in art attained by Michelangelo solidifies his triumph over the past. This surpassing of the past further echoed Vasari's Florentine panegyric of Tuscan cultural achievements. Vasari's classical paralleling is explicit. Indeed, he modelled his art history on the Pliny the Elder's *Natural History* (77–79) but, of course, in Vasari's humanist adaptation of it, Florence and its artists were considered a superior version of the ancient world because of their Christian underpinning.

Vasari's narrative of rebirth took place within a Christian framework, thus offering a convincing argument for Florence's singular superiority in the arts. As part of his Christian worldview, Vasari understood Tuscan achievement in cosmological and eschatological terms, with Florence (and Florentine artists) at the centre of the earth and indeed central to God's greater salvific plan. It was through their deeds and skill that the mysteries of the divine plan were revealed to humanity. In a neo-Platonic way, they stood as imperfect signposts of the perfection of God. According to the Vasarian narrative, perfection in art in the sixteenth century was only possible through a Christian "spark" where the truth of the Creator's greater cosmos—its perfection, longevity, and existence beyond time—was being slowly revealed to man through engagement in creation. Such a privilege was exclusive to Christians.

Thus, the great artists of Greece and Rome would always be subordinate, never attaining Vasarian perfection. As Vasari states in the *Lives*:

> Thus, the first model from which the first image of man arose was a clod of earth, and not without reason, for the Divine Architect of time and of nature, being all perfection, wished to demonstrate, in the imperfection of His materials, what could be done to improve them, just as good sculptors and painters are in the habit of doing, when, by adding additional touches and removing blemishes, they bring their imperfect sketches to such a state of completion and of perfection as they desire.[16]

This Platonic concept of the Prime Mover as craftsman or *artifex maximus* recalls Christian evocations of God as Deus Faber, the divine craftsman and creator of the world.[17]

The Vasarian notion of historical consciousness interprets these ontological phenomena of the starting point of the world as, according to Ulrich Libbrecht, a "real but imperfect becoming."[18] From the humanist perspective, the man-artist is a shadow of the perfect Deus Faber. Thus, all man-made precedents imitating nature represent the imperfections of reality. These imperfections are in constant need of refinement or revision. The humanist project of "imitating" and "restoring" the great but imperfect ancient art forms was essential to attaining a state of near "perfection" which, in Vasari's view, was most diligently expressed in the art of his own time and city. For Vasari, "our art consists entirely of imitation, first of Nature, and then, as it cannot rise so high of itself, of those things which are produced from the masters with the greatest reputation."[19] Because of their Christian beliefs and God's alleged partiality for them, Florentine artists in particular saw their role as the privileged recipients of God's cosmic message, and it is they who constantly strived through the process of imitation to reach perfection. The Vasarian *rinascita* paradigm thus became essentially self-aggrandising in its aim, glorifying Florence as the pinnacle of God's creation as witnessed through the "perfection [of] the art . . . among the Tuscans."[20]

This construct of progress in the arts allowed Vasari to construct a powerful cultural discourse. In order to make sense of the rebirth of the classical arts in his own time Vasari needed to convincingly connect the past with the present.[21] His narrative relies on contemporary historical consciousness to make the claim to the cultural triumph of his time—that is, to identify Florence as the pinnacle of artistic evolution.

Vasari's definition of *rinascita*, therefore, is multidimensional. First, he argues that the rebirth of art was a slow evolutionary progression that was clearly discernible in the arts of painting, sculpture, and architecture. The perfection entailed engaging in a number of developmental stages: *imitazione* and *adeguazione* of the past in order to reach a state of perfection in the sixteenth century. Surpassing the past, the final stage of the *rinascita*, was tied inexorably to God's cosmic plan for the world which He, in Vasari's view, invested in the wholly Christianised Republic of Florence.

Historiography: The nineteenth century, nationalism and colonialism

From the Vasarian perspective the perceived superiority of painting, sculpture, and architecture and the consequent inferior status of the fine arts impacted Western perceptions of all so-called minor arts in the West like tapestries, ceramics, and gold smithing. This also had an impact on Islamic artistic expression. As Denny states that:

> ... once understood, it not only opens up new horizons of artistic accomplishment to our eyes, but in effect liberates us from the straitjacket of the European 'fine arts' mentality that for five centuries has decreed the primacy of painting, sculpture, and architecture, and the inferior status of everything else.[22]

As part of that discourse, painting, sculpture and architecture continued to reign supreme. This perception of inferior status of the fine arts may explain one of the reasons for the lack of receptivity of Ottoman art in the West.

By the seventeenth century, perceptions of the 'Other' in the orientalist discourse led Gottfried Wilhelm Leibniz (1646–1716) to acknowledge the lack of receptivity of the Ottoman civilisation. He described Ottoman lands as places:

[where the a]rts are not honoured; the inhabitants make no effort to improve cultivation of the land, nor do they attempt to build structures that might endure.[23]

In the nineteenth century Leroy-Bealieu, a stanch supporter of European imperialist ambitions, boasts about European greatness having attained civilisational maturity and strength through its colonial ventures. For Leroy-Bealieu such global significance is limited to only 'civilised people'.[24] These political and cultural views resonated within the Renaissance paradigm defined by Vasari in the sixteenth century, exemplifying European achievements. Continuing to reinvent and adapt itself to different times, the *rinascita* of Vasari thus took on a more nationalistic fervour with the emergence of modern European consciousness. The anachronistic application of the Vasarian 'rebirth' paradigm in the nineteenth century made the Renaissance an exclusive pan-European phenomenon. When Jules Michelet and Jacob Burckhardt applied the term 'Renaissance' only to French and Italian experience respectively they were writing history from a perspective that took Europe's position of global dominance as an ultimate truth. Both men saw France and Italy as the quintessential spiritual and creative triumph of European history and the Vasarian paradigm thus became easily malleable to their worldview.[25]

Nineteenth century egalitarian principles of the French Revolution were deeply rooted in his understanding of the term 'Renaissance'. For Michelet, the 'Renaissance' meant:

> [...] the discovery of the world and the discovery of man. The sixteenth century ... went from Columbus to Copernicus, from Copernicus to Galileo, from the discovery of the earth to that of the heavens. Man refound himself.[26]

According to Michelet, the Renaissance represented nineteenth century values like Reason, Truth, Art, and Beauty. Michelet became the first modern thinker to define the Renaissance as a decisive historical period in which a crucial break with the Middle Ages took place in European culture. But, for Michelet, the Renaissance happened in France in the sixteenth century and not in the fourteenth and fifteenth centuries Italy. Brotton claims that:

> [a]s a French nationalist, Michelet was eager to claim the Renaissance as a French phenomenon. As a republican, he also rejected what he saw as fourteenth century Italy's admiration for church and political tyranny as deeply undemocratic, and hence excluded these from the spirit of the Renaissance.[27]

For Michelet, the French Revolution was a key moment in history where the birth of the secular French nation brought the country from the darkness of medievalism to enlightenment.

While Michelet saw France as the centre of European Renaissance, the Swiss historian Jacob Burckhardt defined it as a fifteenth-century Italian phenomenon. In 1860 Burckhardt published his view on history with *The Civilisation of the Renaissance in Italy*. Burckhardt saw the Italian Renaissance as a culture in transition. For him, the Renaissance was the birthplace of modern Europe. He described the Italian Renaissance as 'the mother of our own [age] ... whose influence is still at work'.[28] The role of the individual in Renaissance society was important for Burckhardt, who was writing at the time of the unification of Italy, which was becoming a nation for the first time thus influencing him to form a nationalist framework for the Renaissance.

With the birth of the Eurocentric Renaissance, Burckhardt, like Vasari, made no room for 'the Other'. The Renaissance was defined as an exclusively European phenomenon. It was Italy that gave birth to 'Renaissance Man', who was what Burckhardt called 'the firstborn among the sons of modern Europe'.[29] For later historians, Wallace K. Ferguson and Martin L. McLaughlin, however, the view of the Renaissance as having ushered in the era of modernity occurred much later:

> Confined at first to a rebirth of art or of classical culture, the notion of the Renaissance was broadened as scholars of each successive generation added to it what they regarded as the essence of modern, as opposed to medieval civilization. [30]

Nineteenth-century scholars and thinkers located 'evidence' of the modern in the Renaissance past, tracing the great aspects convincingly to their own day. Their desire to cast the achievements of Renaissance civilisation within a nationalist framework as the epitome of human accomplishments (that is, their accomplishments) has caused problems in art historical discourse and neglected the shared cultural values in the Mediterranean basin.[31]

Orientalism and 'the Other'

If nineteenth century Renaissance discourses encouraged a general disregard of non-European cultural achievements, Orientalism proved even more problematic. The Orient was a framework created by Europeans, which enabled them to view themselves as superior to the Eastern 'Other'. With the publication of Edward Said's *Orientalism* in 1978 the term has become more prevalent in academic discourse of cultural theorists. According to Said:

[I]ndeed it can be argued that the major component in European culture is precisely what made that culture hegemonic both in and outside Europe: the idea of European identity as a superior one in comparison with all the non-European peoples and cultures ... In a quite constant way, Orientalism depends for its strategy on this flexible positional superiority, which puts the Westerner in a whole series of possible relationships with the Orient without ever losing him the relative upper hand.[32]

The imposition of cultural imperialism enforced upon the societies of the Near East reinforces Said's idea of the cultural hegemony that politically justifies Western imperialism and domination. Cultural imperialism represents non-European societies as culturally static and underdeveloped, thereby forcing them to be dependent on the Europeans to become 'civilised' and 'educated.' The fabrication of this cultural superiority means that the 'Other' can be studied, depicted, and reproduced from a European perspective. Indeed, art historian Erwin Panofsky criticised historians for not showing 'professional interest in the aesthetic aspects of civilisation' – i.e. all civilisations.[33] This rebuke underscores the academic neglect of the achievements of the 'Other'. According to Brotton:

Renaissance Europe defined and measured itself in relation to the wealth and splendour of the east, a fact that has been overlooked due to the influence of the nineteenth-century version of the Renaissance until recently.[34]

The cultural imperialism of Orientalist narratives allowed the creation of the 'civilisational Other' to justify and legitimise global domination through European colonialism. In the name of modernity, progress, and cultural superiority, cultural imperialism has contributed to the alienation and marginalisation of non-European cultural achievements.

The growing orientalist literature produced by travellers to the Ottoman Empire and the Orient from the sixteenth century onwards also contributed to the marginalisation of the Ottoman 'Other' and stunted the West's reception of Ottoman art. However, according to Edward Said, any European interest in Islam and the Ottomans was not the result of natural curiosity but rather was based in fear about the 'threats' posed by the Muslim 'Other'.[35] Paradoxically, some Europeans actually admired the military power of the Ottomans, but this had little impact on the historiography. Some visitors to the Ottoman Empire published accounts of their voyages, and descriptions of the lands of the 'Other' in writing, illustrations and paintings. According to Ziauddin Sardar their tales 'about Orientalism' contained nothing that was 'neutral or objective'. Sardar believes that '[b]y definition it is a partial and partisan subject'.[36] For Sardar the Orient that was closest to Europe attained the character that ultimately marked all the other Orients.[37] Without the Ottoman Turks there would not have been orientalism, just as the Crusades would have been unthinkable without Islam in the Middle Ages. Similarly, Claire Norton asserts:

As such the Ottoman Empire is figured as a quintessential Islamic, oriental, or Asian empire, where such terms carry the frequently pejorative connotations common in orientalist discourse ... Very little attention has therefore been given to the extent to which the Ottoman Empire benefited from, participated in and contributed to [via its cultural tradition], what, has been categorised and defined as the Renaissance.[38]

The ambivalent perceptions of the Orientalist therefore perpetuated an indifferent approach to Ottomans' own contributions to the Renaissance discourse. This critical distance between East and West, between the *civilised* and *non-civilised*, is further explored by postcolonial discourse. Like that of Said's *Orientalism*, postcolonial explanations problematise the Renaissance, arguing that foreign cultures can never be presented objectively because of the mediation impacts of language, power and appropriation.[39] According to Stuart Hill:

> [...] power produces new discourses, new kinds of knowledge (i.e. Orientalism), new objects of knowledge (the Orient), it shapes new practices (colonization) and institutions (colonial government).[40]

In the context of representation, Hill argues that 'the circularity of power becomes 'especially important' because 'everyone—the powerful and the powerless—is caught up'.[41] By representing the 'Other' through its eyes, the cultural supremacy of an emerging modern Europe dismissed the achievements of its cultural and ideological adversary.

Representing the 'Other' justifies the dominance of the one who is doing the representing. Therefore, the pan-European Renaissance movement, combined with the narrative of Orientalism, cemented the nineteenth-century paradigm of writers like Michelet and Burckhardt. This paradigm declared France and Italy respectively as the quintessential spiritual and creative triumph of European history. In the orientalist narratives of Michelet and Burckhardt, the Ottoman Empire had no place and was merely perceived as a menace—an alien society. Gerald MacClean sums up the challenging and problematic nature of the nineteenth century construct of the Renaissance as follows:

> If the nineteenth century needed to historicise the artistic achievements of fourteenth- and fifteenth-century Italy by declaring them to signal a rebirth of European magnificence and civilisation, it also needed to ignore the great civilising achievements of the Ottomans by viewing that empire as it were a latter-day version of Rome, doomed to decay and fall.[42]

This review of the impact of Renaissance and Orientalist historiography demonstrates the need for this re-examination of early modern Ottoman art. Although sharing some similar traits with their other Renaissance counterparts, namely with Italy, with the emphasis on the East rather than the classical West, this discussion argues that the Ottomans forged their distinct and separate cultural rebirth in the early modern period. In this way, I argue for an Ottoman rebirth that was different from other contemporaneous renaissances in the Mediterranean, not inferior. Removing the nineteenth-century Eurocentric Renaissance gloss and integrating Vasari's ideas of art as cultural *progress* into a more culturally inclusive narrative allows the exploration of different instances of rebirth with specific and separate characteristics, as expressed by Burioni and Brotton above. In this way, my inclusion of the 'great civilising achievements' of the 'Other' in the Renaissance narrative will both support Necipoğlu's call for 'a fresh narrative' and invite art historians to consider the Renaissance accomplishments of the Ottomans.

Modern revisionist historiography

From the late 1990s revisionist historians began pointing out the problematic nature of orientalism and called for a more inclusive approach to the early modern period. In *Global Interest: Renaissance Art Between East and West*, Lisa Jardine and Jerry Brotton challenge Edward Said's problematic theory of orientalism by negating Said's dominant binary construction of 'us' and 'them'. Jardine and Brotton argue that:

> [...] such arguments enable us to circumvent an account of the marginalized, exoticized, dangerous East within the Renaissance studies as not only politically unhelpful but also historically inaccurate.[43]

Where Said's *Orientalism* problematised the relationship between East and West, Jardine and Brotton moved toward dissolving boundaries and instead argued for the existence of a more receptive interactive experience between East and West.[44] They suggested that once this oppositional orientalist narrative was dismantled, it would negate the belief in 'the antithetical, dark, dirty, exotic, Eastern Other as the negative to which that humane individualism has been opposed—the other ostensibly held at bay by its constructed version of civilization.'[45] This is how modern historiography is addressing the Renaissance and is an approach, which directly underpins this discussion.

Jardine also explores this notion of a broader, shared Renaissance in another work, *Worldly Goods: A New History of the Renaissance*. She looks at the material culture of 'the Age' when Renaissance culture in Italy stretched from its western borders in Christendom to the eastern reaches of the Islamic Ottoman Empire, 'bringing this opulent epoch to life in all its material splendor and competitive acquisitiveness'.[46]

The contribution of such revisionist discourse to re-evaluating east-west interaction in the period remains invaluable, however it only focuses on the influence of the East's material culture on the West. It sees the East's contributions to the Renaissance as merely stimulating the creation, production and promulgation of such objects of cultural exchange. Deborah Howard's efforts to illustrate how Islamic elements have been appropriated into Venetian narratives stresses the impact that the former had on the latter but fails to explore the reverse argument. Instead, she addresses broader issues that arose from the material exchanges that contributed hybrid works and shared cultural inheritances in the early modern period of the Mediterranean.

Such reconciliatory efforts to dissolve boundaries can only improve the art history debate and move the discourse toward a more objective analysis of the art of the 'Other'. Yet this can only be achieved by recognising these material objects as products of vibrant and dynamic societies that had themselves undergone a period of transformation, revival and renewal. According to Deborah Howard, '[t]he concept of East and West remains fundamental to our political, ideological and cultural framework.' [47] Culturally-inclusive approaches to the revisionist debate underscore the continual interest in the notion of Renaissance and the ongoing research needed to recognise the many 'Renaissances throughout the regions, each with their own highly specific and separate characteristics' and to acknowledge 'a wider variety of instances of rebirth'.[48]

Recent work by Rosamond Mack, *Bazaar to Piazza: Islamic Trade and Italian Art, 1300–1600,* is part of a growing body of scholarly work that focuses on the artistic exchanges that occurred during the Renaissance in the Mediterranean basin, through trade in non-figurative goods (e.g. carpets, ceramics and silks). Whilst existing work already suggests that artistic exchange occurred in the medieval period, Mack extends the narrative by asserting that these artistic exchanges also occurred in Renaissance Italy. In doing so, Mack challenges the traditional view that Renaissance artistic achievements were a self-contained phenomenon. Thus, in Italy, a hybrid form of artistic production emerged but Mack does not view this as having hindered the cultural blossoming of either (western European or Ottoman) Renaissances. In fact, Mack concludes her book by writing, '[s]ixteenth century East–West trade and artistic exchange softened a clash of civilizations, establishing a historical precedent for cultural coexistence and mutual enrichment.'[49] This is a point firmly held by this discussion.

Luxury objects and their exchange certainly became part and parcel of elite and merchant life of both East and West. Both cultures depended on such exchange. In fact, trade was the life-blood of not only European life but of Mediterranean life more generally in the global Renaissance. It is this cultural coexistence that provided the fluidity of the Renaissance age and which demands a broader Renaissance purview. Such artistic and cultural exchanges—through diplomatic, commercial, and of course, military means—gave the Ottomans from the fifteenth century onwards the opportunities to be influenced not just by the legacy of the West but also by the classical heritage of the Islamic East. The impact of such exchanges influenced the visual expressions of its court culture beyond its borders in Eastern and Western Europe. Thus, the broader understanding of the Renaissance goes beyond the parameters of the Mediterranean and seeks to find a holistic explanation of the Ottoman Renaissance in the Ottoman's own meaningful context. Although important, the Ottoman Renaissance does not stop at the revival of ancient Greek and Roman ideals, or its interaction with the West. In response to an obvious lacuna in the literature, this explores explores the cultural, political and religious ties to the Ottomans' Eastern predecessors as well to demonstrate a larger context for the early modern Renaissance. Such an approach undermines the notion of *rinascita* and nineteenth-century Eurocentric perceptions of the age. By extending the contemporary historiographical discussion to previously excluded, yet intimately connected, others, the research uniquely highlights both the Eastern and Western legacy of the Ottoman Renaissance, and it brings to the fore the truly global nature of the early modern experience.

Indeed, the notion of an Ottoman Renaissance has been suggested before. Late nineteenth and early twentieth-century architectural historians acknowledged the notion of an Ottoman Renaissance in the fifteenth and sixteenth centuries. As early as 1874, German architect Friedrich Adler acknowledged the 'spatial unity' and 'purist character' of Ottoman architecture.[50] As early as 1907 the idea of a Turkish Renaissance emerged, initiated by the German art historian and architect Cornelius Gurlitt, who recognised the originality of Ottoman architecture and the creative genius of Sinan and placed both within the Renaissance paradigm.[51] Gurlitt in fact dismissed the common idea that Ottoman architecture was a mere imitation of the Hagia Sophia and recognised instead that it was a product of a shared Mediterranean legacy or *zeitgeist* (spirit of the age):

We have been enthusiastic in our praise of Italy, a country that at the end of the fifteenth century resurrected the art of ancient Rome after this achievement had lain dormant for over a thousand years. During the same period, however, buildings were erected on the Bosphorus that have been belittled for the simple reason that they were replicas of Hagia Sophia. Yet it is no less a renaissance of astounding individuality that sprang up from the soil made fertile by the spirit of ancient Greece. The revival of ancient perceptions of shape and form occurred here with the same freedom, independence, and boldness, with the same artistic and creative force, that was shaping the culture on the opposite shores of the Adriatic Sea.[52]

Gurlitt argues that the free sharing and fusing of cultural values shaped the sixteenth century cultural revivalism of the Mediterranean basin of which the Ottomans were also significant participants. The uniqueness of Gurlitt's early view of Ottoman art has only been taken up recently.

Building on the work of Cornelius Gurlitt, in 1914 the German orientalist Franz Babinger, in an article titled 'Die türkische Renaissance' (The Turkish Renaissance), compared Sinan's central plan domed mosques to the works of Bramante, Giuliano da Sangallo, Baldassare Peruzzi, and Michelangelo Buonarotti.[53] A year later Babinger even gave Sinan the sobriquet 'the Ottoman Michelangelo'.[54] The aim of his two articles was merely to invite historians and art historians to collaborate in bringing Sinan's works to universal recognition. His invitation was therefore like Necipoğlu's call for a 'fresh narrative'. Babinger recognised that Sinan's imperial architectural monuments and also the aesthetic decorative styles of Ottoman fine arts were products sparked by the same Renaissance spirit of curiosity and competitiveness that exemplified the period elsewhere in Europe.

By 1925 Glück, in collaboration with Ernest Diez, produced *Die Kunst des Islam* which further elaborated the theory of the Turkish Renaissance. Diez later argued that the Ottoman dynasty needed monumental 'architectural representation' like the Romans.[55] He went on to emphasise the cross-cultural heritage of Ottoman and Italian Renaissance architecture in the Roman imperial tradition and attributed their similarities to a 'period style'. He called this style, *'Zeitstil'*.[56] Turkish historian Halil Inalcik who in 1973 published *The Ottoman Empire: The Classical Age 1300–1600* reached the same conclusion; that is, that the Ottoman imperial state architecture is not authentically Turkish but rather a product of past and present exemplars from Roman/Byzantine, Islamic, and Timurid-Persianate-Turkic traditions from Central Asia.[57] Furthermore, in 1986 art historian Esin Atıl concurred with the view that, like its architecture, Ottoman art of the fifteenth and sixteenth centuries 'saw the synthesis of European, Islamic and Turkish traditions and the creation of an artistic vocabulary that was unique to the Ottoman world'.[58] The result of a shared heritage by the Ottomans produced unique art mediums from the monumental religious to secular works of art including tiles, calligraphy, illustrated manuscripts, ceramics, carpets, and embroidered textiles. Combined with its ceremonials and pageants they reflected the power of the visual tastes of the sultan's court.

While Diez, Inalcık and Atıl argue that the Ottoman aesthetic is the product of a cultural fusion - this discussion goes further. It considers that at the core of the Ottoman aesthetic lay an underlying Renaissance mindset—one that was conscious of its historical legacy and global supremacy, and was determined to overcome the technological and engineering challenges it faced. With this conviction, visual representations of its ruling elite constructed a distinct early modern cultural identity through strategic imitation, adaptation and perfection (or surpassing) of their own cultural legacies. This distinct identity set the Ottoman aesthetic apart from its Eastern 'cousins'.

Despite some positive assessments of Ottoman art during the late nineteenth and early twentieth centuries, scholarly works produced in the latter decades of the twentieth century continued the ambivalent attitudes to early modern Ottoman achievements. Turkish architectural historian Doğan Kuban in his work *Ottoman Architecture* focuses on the functionality and practical aspects of Ottoman imperial mosques. While considering the complexity, architectural detail and workmanship, Kuban dismisses the notion that there was a rebirth in this area in the fifteenth and sixteenth centuries.[59] Further rejecting the Renaissance mindset of Sinan, one of his main claims is that treatises comparable to those in the West which set the standard for European architects, were not produced by Ottoman architects and other intellectuals in the East. Necipoğlu, however, finds this discourse very problematic because according to her 'it assumes that any kind of theoretical approach requires a Vitrivian written manifestation, whereas one can argue that, in Ottoman culture, certain aspects remained part of oral culture, and that written culture remained in a different manner'.[60] According to her this does not in any way prove that the Ottoman architects, including Sinan and other artisans, did not have a theory in mind. Other Ottoman architectural historians, including Godfrey Goodwin in his 1971 work *A History of Ottoman Architecture*, attempt to bring a balance to the debate. Goodwin states that the purpose of his work on Ottoman architecture is to demonstrate that 'far from being a merely a decadent mixture of Persian, Byzantine and other styles...' Ottoman architecture '... is a historic style in its own right.'[61] Although acknowledging the uniqueness of Ottoman art, Goodwin, like Kuban is also reluctant to engage in the notion of an early modern Ottoman Renaissance. Moreover, art historian Walter B. Denny, in his work *Iznik: The Artistry of Ottoman Ceramics,* asserts that the Ottomans made one of their greatest artistic contributions in early modern ceramic technology that 'reflected the fundamental design medium for Ottoman art.'[62] Atasoy and Atıl similarly affirm the creativity of early modern Ottoman fine arts.[63] It is at this point where this discussion builds on the previous works to bring to the fore the distinctive nature and character of the Ottoman Renaissance.

In her 2004 work, *Creating East and West: Renaissance Humanists and the Ottoman Turks*, in an epilogue entitled, 'The Renaissance Legacy', Nancy Bisaha acknowledges that Western views are still influenced by Renaissance humanist responses to the Ottoman Turks.[64] Despite the fact that Renaissance humanists cultivated a further understanding of Muslim culture and religion, they also fostered the 'hostile take on the Ottoman Turks', which 'only served to nurture incipient ideas of Western superiority to Eastern rivals'.[65] Indeed, Western historiography is still somewhat indecisive about the Ottomans, with scholars and academics still constrained by the traditionalist Renaissance legacy. They do not see the rebirth of Ottoman art on its own cultural merits. The core of this indecisiveness is seen by some as stemming from the centuries during which Europe faced the Ottoman threat.[66] As a consequence, the cultural expressions of the Ottomans were simply overlooked and not taken very seriously. Yet, there remain significant challenges to this viewpoint. For instance, Stephane Yerasimos states in relation to the Süleymaniye Mosque in Istanbul that '[i]t is interesting to observe how, in a mind as creative as Sinan's, an obsessive dialogue with a model can evolve into a path toward genuine originality'.[67] Art historians whose analyses have not taken account of his innovative style have misrepresented Sinan's mosque designs, which used a central dome flanked by two half-domes. According to Besnier-Kılıçoğlu, Sinan's 'failure to recognize the continuous development of syntactical conceptual methodology leads them to see the Süleymaniye Mosque as a copy of the sixth-century Byzantine basilica of Hagia Sophia'.[68] Rather than see his work as mere copies, many modern historians view Sinan's work as a meaningful fusion of Turkish and Byzantine elements, which together produce a distinctly Ottoman style. Instead, Sinan's distinctly early modern Ottoman style needs to be seen as one that 'perfects' the past exemplars and gives it rebirth in a new Ottoman cultural setting. In this way, his works are seen in the broader context of a growing empire, as complementing Ottoman expressions of ceremonial and political power, authority and universal legitimacy in an age where imperial rivalries in the Mediterranean competed with one another for regional and global supremacy.

Although Burckhardt's dream of a Renaissance civilisation in Italy has been revised by recent scholarship, Guido Ruggiero notes that the term Renaissance "seems continually to return, adapting itself to changing times'.[69] It is, therefore, natural to broaden the term beyond the confines of the Italo-centric narrative to include the Ottoman art of the early modern period. Indeed, by interrogating the Ottoman voice from the sixteenth-century historical context—Sinan—the need for this broader understanding becomes even more apparent.

Sinan's 'azim (magnificence)

In 2005, Gülru Necipoğlu published a ground-breaking study on the Ottoman Renaissance architect Sinan. In the text, she analysed the great buildings and aesthetics of Sinan, placing his accomplishments fully within his own historical period. In short, she deftly scrutinised Sinan's works within a broader framework that connected the past to the present and the local to the global. She noted his adherence to past models as well as his Sufi humanist values. In doing so she presented an inspiring model for future Ottoman studies. In her text, Necipoğlu called for 'a "fresh narrative" [to] rescue [Ottoman arts] from the clichés of orientalist theories and to set it into a more universal historical perspective."[70] Focusing on cultural appropriation of classical works, according to Soyini Madison "involves an intertextual process of creating or revisioning an object, idea, or subject from another object, idea, or subject to create another or different version."[71] Cultural appropriation does not intend to imitate or mimic, "or to necessarily make it known that appropriation has even taken place or to reveal that in creating this new form something has been borrowed."[72] In the context of Ottoman architecture, sixteenth-century imperial architect Sinan boastfully states in his autobiographies that he triumphed over the Roman/Byzantine Hagia Sophia by creating the largest dome the world had ever seen at the time, clearly demonstrating the competitive spirit of the age and the creation of a new, distinct artistic medium.[73]

Like his Renaissance contemporaries, Sinan composed his treatise ". . . in order that a memorial and record [of his artworks] endure through the pages of time."[74] The treatise lists all his works—mosques, hospices, madrasas, bridges, palaces, fountains, and countless other structures—as a testimony of the decades of learning and adapting of the old into something new in the creation of a distinct Ottoman style. Sinan states:

I acquired a sought-after bit of wisdom from the crenellation of great ancient remains and a provision of knowledge from every ruined monument.[75]

Having learned from the ancient ruins around him by *tecdid* (restoring, renovating and renewing), he refined his *sūret*, *üsl'ub* (style) and gave birth to the old.[76] Sinan attained *'azim* (magnificence), *nezāket* (elegance, refinement), *cemile* (beauty), and *zuhūrat*, literally meaning perfection, through stylistic progression in his buildings leading to his distinct new *sūret*.[77] Like Vasari and Ali, Sinan saw a linear progress in his work. "Day by day many types of buildings [are created], and refinement increased," he writes, signifying the progression of art through the ages and its culmination in "complete realization."[78] Praising his 1548 work, the Şehzade Mosque, in the style of the Hagia Sophia in Istanbul, Sinan confirms, "such artistry had not been previously accomplished by any master," as previous works imitating the *Ayasōfya tarzı[nda]* (Hagia Sophia style) "did not possess elegance."[79] Sinan informs the reader that the Roman/Byzantine structure of the *Ayasōfya tarzı[nda]* became the inspiration for his works and that these works in return became a *nūmūne* (model) for the Süleymaniye Mosque (1557–8): "this servant perfected the noble Friday mosque of Şehzade Sultan Mehmed . . . in the style of Hagia Sophia . . . which was the model for the model building complex of His Majesty Sultan Süleyman Khan."[80] To signify the rebirth of the classical past exemplified in the Süleymaniye Mosque, Sinan refers to "four marble columns" used in the construction of the building.[81] Like St. Peter's "stone columns" coming from Roman antiquity "the mold of Hadrian" according to Vasari, each of Sinan's four marble columns came from different parts of the empire.[82] He states:

Each of its variegated marbles was removed to the horizon and came as a token from a different land. According to most historians they were left from the palace of His Majesty Solomon's Belkis [Queen of Sheba] . . . Also another brought from Alexandria with a base . . . another column [i.e. from the remnants of the old Byzantine Palace] was found standing ready in the imperial palace [Topkapı Palace], [and the] Maiden's Column [from the Church of the Holy Apostles in Istanbul].[83]

The symbolism surely was not lost on Süleyman. The columns alluded to the following: biblical figure Solomon, the namesake of Sultan Süleyman, ancient Egypt, the Eastern Roman emperors, and Christianity, demonstrating the Ottoman dominance of these civilizations under Süleyman. According to Selen B. Morkoç, the use of marble columns from Istanbul and other parts of the empire alludes to "[. . .] distinct royal connotations even if they appeared to be identical."[84] Combined with the Hagia Sophia style, this gave birth to the classical past within an Islamic monument that embraced all the civilizations that had come before it, which allowed Sinan to claim that "[t]he arts manifested in it."[85] Under his guidance the old model of the Hagia Sophia was transformed into a distinctly new Ottoman form in the Süleymaniye and embodied the "'*azim*" of Ottoman cultural greatness. In Spiro Kostof's words the Ottomans were now in a position to "stage their own renaissance."[86]

Concurring with Kostof's line of argument of the links to classical antiquity in the Mediterranean, Necipoğlu also sees parallelisms in architectural aesthetics in Renaissance Italy and in the Ottoman Empire. Byzantine structures displayed an architectural heritage that ran parallel to that of Istanbul and Venice, and was perhaps made even more pronounced by their similar geographies tied to the Mediterranean Sea.[87] Oral and written accounts, as well as drawings by European diplomats and artists, became the media through which Ottoman architecture became more widely known. Michelangelo, for example, while known to have studied the domes of Florence Cathedral, and the Pantheon, he most likely included those of Hagia Sophia and Sinan's Süleymaniye mosque in Istanbul.[88] Similarly, Michelangelo who once contemplated entering the service of Sultan Bajezid II may have collected information about Sinan's mosques and his technology of dome construction—particularly considering that Süleymaniye mosque and St. Peter's Basilica were constructed at around the same period, i.e., between 1548-1557[89] and 1552-1564[90], respectively. In fact, when Pietro della Valle visited Istanbul in 1614, he noticed similarities between the two structures:

[T]hat which is noteworthy are the mosques, in particular four or five of them built by the Turkish emperors, all of them situated on the highest hilltops in such a way that they almost form a row, visible from one end of the sea to the other and equally distributed along the whole length of the city. They are well built in marble and differ little in architecture from one another, being in the form of a temple composed of a domed square, like the design of St. Peter's in Rome by Michelangelo; and I believe they have taken as their model Hagia Sophia which they encountered there.[91]

Pietro della Valle also wrote that he had promised to bring back paintings of Sinan's mosques and the Hagia Sophia, so that Italian architects could use them as sources of inspiration.[92] When Michelangelo took over the project of St Peter's from his predecessors, Bramante and Sangallo, the interior had already been completed. While the original architects had proposed the use of a single-shell dome, Michelangelo's original design opted for spur-like buttresses with paired columns, which alternated with windows and included four smaller domes on each corner. Interestingly, Michelangelo had proposed something very similar to the Hagia Sophia and the mosques of Sinan.[93] While one cannot make any claims with absolute certainty, it is possible that Michelangelo's original design—with its stylistic resemblance to Sinan's mosques—may indicate that he found inspiration in the work of his Ottoman counterpart. However, after Michelangelo's death in 1564, the hemispherical dome that he intended for was modified to resemble the one belonging to Florence Cathedral.

By the middle of the sixteenth century, Sinan had codified the architectural style of the Ottoman mosque and this codification may explain why the influence of Italian architectural innovation began to wane in the East. However, his experimentation did not stop him from learning about Italian architecture, in particular, through his close friendship with the *dragoman* Yunus Bey, who was sent to Venice on diplomatic missions. Such was their friendship that Sinan also built a mosque, in Istanbul, in Bey's honour. It is likely that through connections such as Bey; through oral reports and architectural prints, Sinan would have learned of the construction of St. Peter's in Rome. As a side note, the plans for the build were once kept at the office of royal architects at Vefa, in Istanbul, but have since been lost. However, certain French embassy letters from the eighteenth century report of Sultan Mahmud

I's chief architect having, at his disposal, a collection of prints and plans—including a Turkish translation of the treatise of architecture.[94] Francesco Dei Marchi also mentions Ottoman travellers who, during the 1540s, saw St. Peter's Basilica:

[T]he temple of S. Pietro in Rome is the most magnificent in all of Christendom, and when it is built according to the design and model none other like it will be found anywhere [...] and certainly all men on earth desire that this temple should be completed and seek to aid and favor its completion, even including the Turks, enemies of the true faith. I spoke with some of them in Rome, who desired that this Church may be finished according to its beautiful and marvellous beginnings.[95]

Therefore, it is possible that Sinan also had access to Italian plans that were carried by returning Ottoman travellers. Additionally, Burns suggests that Antonio Salamanca's engravings of Sangallo's wooden model of St Peter's may have been available to Sinan, which could explain the more complex piers of the Süleymaniye mosque (*Figures 3, 4*).[96]

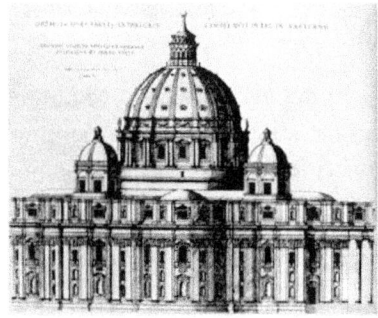 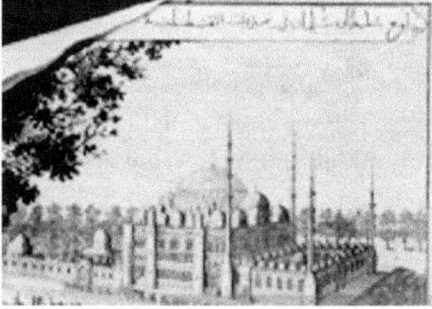

Figures 3, 4. Left, Michelangelo, elevation of the exterior of St. Peter's in an engraving by Antonio Salamanca, 1547; right, 18th century engraving of the Süleymaniye Mosque, Fischer von Erlach, 1721. Photograph reproductions.

While one can only speculate on Sinan's level of access to, and awareness of, designs for St. Peter's it is noteworthy that he decided to revise
the façade of his masterpiece, the Selimiye mosque in Edirne (1569-75).
By abandoning the mosque's pyramidal cascade of domes and intro-
ducing a lateral façade, in order to balance its horizontal tiers, the
mosque became more similar to Michelangelo's church in Rome, and
Alberti's Santa Maria Novella in Florence (*Figures 5, 6*).

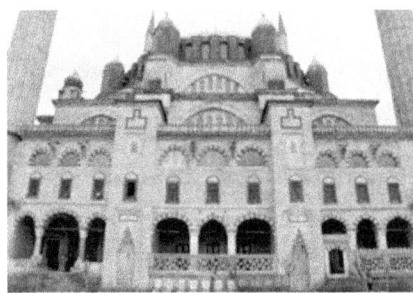 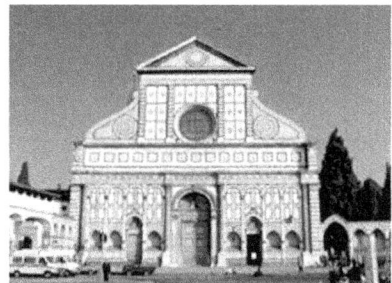

*Figures 5, 6. Left, the geometric designs of the façade of the Selimiye (1575).
Photograph by Metin Mustafa, December, 2014; right, façade of Santa Maria
Novella completed by Alberti in 1470. Photograph by M. Aksoy, June, 2011.*

The updated Selimiye façade, which reflects Renaissance aesthetics,
demonstrates that the similarities on both sides of the Mediterranean
may have been due to cross-cultural exchanges of idea—through oral
and written reports, and architectural prints.

The relationship with classical antiquity in the early modern Mediterranean civilisations with Sinan's architecture is valuable in re-orienting
our understanding of the Renaissance. This affinity represents the
"relationships among world civilisations freed from the Western-
Eastern stereotypes and hierarchies" and reinforces Necipoğlu's call
for a "fresh narrative".[97]

Sinan's self-aggrandising tone in relation to his achievement in the
Süleymaniye reflects the spirit of the Renaissance. It also embodies his
claim that such monumental representation was a reflection of a global
ruler like Süleyman. As David Lowenthal claims, "[a] magnified or
invented antiquity also aggrandizes localities and individuals."[98] The

visual metaphor of the Süleymaniye Mosque established the universal status of Süleyman, while the city of Istanbul gained the crowning glory of Ottoman imperialism. Necipoğlu asserts that the Süleymaniye complex "[. . .] demonstrate[s] that culturally recognized symbolic and ideological [political and religious] associations . . . constitute[s] a significant aspect of the Süleymaniye's multilayered architectural discourse."[99] By resurrecting these four columns of antiquity within the context of the sixteenth century, Sinan emphasises the early modern nature of Ottoman historical consciousness. This under-standing resonates with Jörn Rüsen's theory of the lasting legacy of historical consciousness: "Historical consciousness specifically does not reduce the meaningful and sense bearing time to just the past, rather . . . historical memory will always and fundamentally have a perspective of the present and the future." [100] Vasari had noted that Florentine artists in 1013 learned from classical works by imitating "the good ancient order in the doors, windows, columns, arches and cornices, which they perceived in part in the very ancient church of San Giovanni."[101] In the subsequent centuries, their art reached its status of *perfezione*, that is, its "great" and "truly extraordinary beauty" with Michelangelo. Similarly, Sinan, like his Italian counterpart, attained '*azim* (magnificence), *nezāket* (elegance, refinement), and *cemile* (beauty). Each of his art works—mosques, minarets, mihrabs, minbars, fountains—were like the Tuscan creations, "each of them matchlessly furnished" having "attained perfection" in the years after the Abbasids.[102]

This attainment of '*azim* strongly reflects the influence that the humanist interest in ancient Greece had on the Ottomans. For example, the idea of magnificence, imbued in the architecture of Sinan, aligns with Aristotelian notions of magnificence expressed in the *Nicomachean Ethics*. Here, "the greatness implied in the name of the magnificent man [...] will produce a more magnificent work of art."[103] Like Aristo-tle's notion of magnificence, Sinan's '*azim* also attains an aesthetic dimension. For Sinan, this state of *zuhūrat* (perfection) and *a'zam* came to fruition in his own lifetime and under his own artistic guidance, recalling Vasari's claim that (European) art reached perfection in his own time. It can therefore be argued that it is at this meeting point that the two dominant civilisations of the sixteenth century, Italy and the Ottoman Empire, usher in the Mediterranean *zeitgeist* that produce works of art reinforcing Cornelius Gurlitt's words above. Before comparing the uniqueness of the interior decorative aesthetics of the Rustem Pasha Mosque of Sinan with Michelangelo's *Last Judgement*, it is pertinent to gain understanding of the influence of Sufi humanism on Islamic and Ottoman art, and more specifically – on Sinan's aesthetics.

CHAPTER 2

SUFI HUMANISM AND ISLAMIC ART

Islamic art provides the observer with a larger view of the Qur'anic paradise through the prism of Sufi mysticism. As Seyyed Hossein Nasr states: "[...] Islamic art [i]s the manifesta-tion in the world of forms of the spiritual realities (al-haqa'iq) of the Islamic revelation itself as coloured by its earthly embodiments."[1] To gain a closer relationship with God, in Sufi philosophy, a number of key themes including: theophanies (visible manifestations of God to humankind), a world which access is given by means of esoteric knowledge through symbols (ta'wil), tawhid (Unity of God), ittihad (Union with God), and the creative imagination are fundamental in understanding the nature of Islamic art aesthetics.[2] Islamic art embodies these key Sufi elements. According to David P. Brewster, '[...] it is ... true to say that Sufism, together with Islamic Art and Architecture, represents one of the more "immediate" and accessible aspects of Islam [...] to Western students [and scholars]."[3] Influence of Sufism is evident on the Ottoman Renaissance thought and visual culture. The theophanic experience imbued by the Ottoman imperial architect Sinan's (d. 1588) aesthetics in his 1575 masterpiece, the Selimiye Mosque in Edirne is a celebration of Sufi humanism. Sinan's scribe, Mustafa Sa'i celebrates this mystical experience of Sinan's achievements in the architect's autobiographies.

Tawhid and Ittihad

Understanding Islamic art requires understanding of the idea of *tawhid*. *Tawhid*, the belief and acknowledgment in the Unity and Oneness of the Indivisible God is paramount. In the Qur'an, God says: "Do not set up besides God any other deity." (17:22) *Ittihad*, on the other hand means to be one with God. According to Seyyed Hossein Nasr:

> Islamic art is the result of the manifestation of Unity upon the plane of multiplicity. It reflects in a blinding manner the Unity of the Divine Principle, the dependence of all multiplicity upon the One, the ephemerality of the world and the positive qualities of cosmic existence or creation about which God asserts in the Quran, 'Our Lord! Thou creates not this in vain.' (111:191)[4]

The comprehension of the *tawhid* for the Sufi and its dependence upon multiplicity requires silence and contemplation. In order to achieve this, Nasr states:

> This art makes manifest, in the physical order directly perceivable by the senses, the archetypal realities and acts, therefore, as a ladder for the journey of the soul from the visible and the audible to the Invisible which is also Silence transcending all sound.[5]

Thus, in a sacred space like the mosque, the experience of silence and contemplation ot the observer activates the senses to perceive the 'archetypal realities' of the hereafter (life without death, disease, illness, and eternal bliss). This serves as a stepping-stone for the soul to comprehend the Unity of God and the knowers verification and cognition of the transcendent Reality and Truth.

For the observer the experience the soul undergoes in a sacred space surrounded by decorative aesthetics become an inner link to his spirituality. As Nasr explains, "[...] this art plays in the induction of *hal* or spiritual state, which is itself a grace from Heaven, and in the attitude of those closest to the heart of Islamic spirituality to this art in its manifold manifestations."[6] Islamic art, as all art aesthetics play on one's senses and emotions for it places emphasis on the 'origin of the inward in the outward and reduces sacred art with its interiorizing power to simply external.'[7] The connection of St Thomas's dictum, '*ars sine sciential nihil*' (the art without science is nothing) to Islamic art is based upon the 'science of nature'.[8] This science is not concerned with the outward appearance of things, but with their inner reality. The visual vocabulary of Iznik naturalism, for example, serve to unlock and stir the inner realities of the self and Hidden One (i.e. God) for art itself is the manifestation of the Beauty of God and His Creation.

In a similar way, to understand Islamic fine art one must also tap into his own spirituality in order to seek *Ittihad* – Union with God. As Şefik Can notes: "The level of *Ittihad* is superior to the level of *tawhid* because in the former there is only the notion of God as one, while in the latter there is the notion of being one with God."[9] Can, as a Sufi scholar explores this concept further indicating that to become one with God, one must enter the path of God to cleanse his lower self (*nafs* of the ego) through 'self-mortification', 'good deeds' and 'worship'.[10] As Algar states:

This Sufism is meditative and ethical. The vision of God is insight into reality; it yields understanding of the self and the place of the self in the world and brings into harmony inner character and outer behaviour.[11]

It is through these actions that the individual can demonstrate his obei-
sance to the One. In doing so the individual submits his free will to
God alone – the individual them, according to Can, has attained God.[12]
On this matter Rumi elaborates further: "If you kill your desires and
do away with your human attributes, the sea of secrets carries you
over its head."[13] For the Sufi, this attainment by the individual makes
him *insan al-kamil* – the ideal human being. According to Rumi:

I do not know how I have become effaced; is it due to that wine of
divine love / Or where I am due to that Beauty of Nowhere? I
arrived at such a place that I do not fit into that world / Now I do
not suit anyone other than Unique Beloved who is not associated
with a place / You are telling me: 'Why aren't you coming to yourself [to your senses] You show to me myself and who I am, and I
shall come to myself. You are the light, you called out to Moses, 'I
am God, I am God!'[14]

However, becoming one with God, the individual cannot stay in that
state indefinitely because he cannot carry the heavy burden. As Rumi
states, 'I cannot sit with You as much as I want as long as Your love
does not empty myself from myself and as long as I do not give up on
myself, my anachronism."[15] As for *tawhid*, for Rumi, it is attainable in
the silence: 'In disciplined silence it opens. With wandering talk it clos-
es."[16] Sinan demonstrates this in his mosques, none more so than in
the Rustem Pasha Mosque. It is in the silence of the ambiance of the
mosque interior surrounded by the art of Iznik tiles that one experiences this spiritual awakening which the next chapter elaborates on
further. However, this spiritual awakening cannot happen without Sufi
esotericism and the allegorical interpretation of the Qur'an (*ta'wil*).

Ta'wil and esoteric knowledge

The Sufi interpretation of the Qur'an is also known as the esoteric
interpretation of the Revelation. For the Sufi, the esoteric interpretation
of the Qur'an establishes a symbolic connection to God and the imag-

ined world - paradise. Through this mystical elucidation, God's Signs (*ayah*) in Nature serve as symbols to attain spiritual knowledge. It is here that the naturalism of Islamic aesthetics becomes tools for the observer to gain knowledge of the self (*nafs*) and reach a higher plane of spirituality in his quest of *tawhid* and *ittihad*. For this reason Nasr states:

> To grasp fully the significance of Islamic art is to become aware that it is an aspect of the Islamic revelation, a casting of the Divine Realities (*haqa'iq*) upon the plane of material manifestation in order to carry man upon the wings of its liberating beauty to his original abode of Divine Proximity.[17]

In order to reach the 'original abode' esoteric interpretation of the scripture requires theophanic understanding of the symbolisms attached to the message it is intended to convey. The symbolisms associated with the material manifestations of God's Beauty can be seen in the Islamic garden imitating the Garden of Eden on earth expressed in the Qur'an where the righteous will have gardens beneath which rivers flow (18:31). In a similar way the symbolisms linked with multitude of flowers in Islamic naturalism allows the individual to:

> [...] see through the phenomena of the natural world in all its intimate glory to the underlying truth: Nature, as a sign of God, both veils and reveals. So the beauty of the natural world is one of God's greatest symbols and through meditation on its glories we can, as with all true sacred art retrace a back to Truth.[18]

For the observer, to make sense of the deeper meaning of his life requires self-reflection, prayer and meditation. The sacred space is one such place providing this theophanic experience through the symbolisms associated with objects – in this case - floral representations of paradise.

Islamic art has been influenced by Sufi humanism and the classical ideals of Plato. It remains unknown whether Rumi had read the works of Plato, but with the existence of medieval Arabic translations of classical works circulating in the Islamic world there is a chance that he may have done so. Rumi, like Plato, sought to find and understand, and make others understand, the Being who created the universe. This role of God is echoed in the Qur'an's descriptions of His attributes: *Al-Khalik* (the Creator 6:102, 13:16), *Al-Musawwir* (the Fashioner of forms 59:24) that manifest in nature, and His ever-forgiving attribute, the *Al-Ghaffar*.[19] Both masters declared that everything living must have origins. Both agreed that our spirits dwelt in some place before our existence came into being on earth. Plato calls this the 'World of Ideas', 'World of Examples', while Rumi and other Sufi scholars call it the 'World of Souls and Lights' (*malakut*) and the 'Imaginal World' (*mithal*). According to Rumi:

[...] our real motherland is that universe which is the 'World of Absolute Beauty.' We are strangers on earth. All human beings are strangers in this world ... We have been exiled from that world into this one.[20]

From this philosophical viewpoint, because humans have been exiled to earth the yearning for beauty and perfection are innate human traits. We are continually in search for these qualities. This yearning for the Hereafter also concurs with the medieval Sufi scholar Yahya Ibn Habash Suhrawardi's (d. 1191) philosophy of illumination. Suhrawardi claims that all creation emanate from the Light of Lights for the Qur'an states:

God is the light of the heavens and the earth. The Parable of His Light is a if there were a Niche and within it a Lamp: the Lamp enclosed in Glass: the glass as it were a brilliant star: lit from a blessed Tree, an Olive, neither of the East nor of the West, whose oil is well-nigh luminous, though fire scarcely touched it: Light upon light …[24:35]

Influenced by Plato and Ibn Sina (Avicenna), Suhrawardi considers a past existence for every soul in the realm of the angels before uniting with the body. For Suhrawardi, there are two parts to the human soul: one part remains in paradise and the other is constricted by the confines of the physical body. From this perspective the human soul always aspires to reunite with its other half in the realm of heaven. This is the only way the soul can find true bliss and happiness.[21] It can therefore be argued that from this perspective, through a theophanic experiencing, the individual gains a glimpse of the Hereafter and access the world of immaterial lights.

Furthermore, Rumi reminds one that everything is not perfect and is subject to permanent change. He reminds one that one should not be troubled about the beauties that perish or decay in this world. Rumi accordingly says:

The original of every substance, or every picture you see in this world is in the World of the Spirit. Do not worry that this picture is gone. Do not be troubled that every pretty face you have seen, every subtle saying you have heard has vanished since the truth does not consist of what you see and what you know in this world.[22]

From this perspective, for Rumi, the individual has been given responsibilities to seek the world to come, the Hereafter, to find salvation and mercy.

For the Sufi, the self's continuous striving for contentment begins with ongoing reflection on one's shortcomings. Influenced by Sufi mysticism, Islamic art and more specifically the Iznik aesthetic echoes Rumi's famous words:

> Come, come, whoever you are. Wanderer, worshiper, lover of leaving. It doesn't matter. Ours is not a caravan of despair. Come, even if you have broken your vows a thousand times. Come, yet again, come, come.[23]

In other words, hope and salvation come with the sincerity and true intentions of the believer who submits to the One, even after a thousand sins. This yearning to seek the One according to Ibn Arabi (1165-1240), the Andalusian Sufi and mystic scholar, is where "[…] the Active Imagination [of the individual] carries out the divine intention, the intention of the 'Hidden Treasure' [i.e. God and His Beauty] yearning to be known […]" because like the observer seeking, He, too, desires to be discovered.[24] The individual ponders on this from the moment of entering a sacred space like a mosque.

Creative Imagination as theophany

The 'Imaginal World' (*mithal*) and World of Souls and Lights (*malakut*) are totally unconnected to matter and the mundane physical reality in the peripatetic sense. For Islamic art, from monumental architecture, miniature paintings to tiles, characteristic of Ottoman, Persian and other Islamic art of the East, according to Nasr is an "[…] echo of the joy of paradise serving as reminders of a reality which transcends the mundane surroundings of human life."[25] It is only through esoteric knowledge and theophanic experience that man is able to penetrate into the meaning of other realms.[26] Concerning this Imaginal World, Suhrawardi's (d. 1191) commentator Qutbuddin Shirazi (d. 1311) says:

It is there that the various kinds of autonomous archetypal Images are infinitely realised, forming a hierarchy of degrees varying according to their relative subtlety or density ... The pilgrim rising from one degree to another discovers on each higher level a subtler state, a more entrancing beauty, a more intense spirituality, a more overflowing delight. The highest of these degrees borders on the intelligible pure entities of Light and very closely resembles it.[27]

In Sufi terminology, these archetypes images consist of the manifestations of the Divine Names in the realm of Knowledge. They symbolise the existential substances or spiritual forms that relate to the origins of eventualities and possibilities. Although the relationships of these spiritual forms seem to be within the frame of time, they are beyond time. According to Ibn Arabi the realisation of these archetypal images and realities requires the use of the Creative Imagination.[28] For the observer in the sacred space searching for meaning and self-transformation, the wandering, contemplation and self-reflection act as a prayer. For Ibn Arabi, prayer:

[...] is the expression of a mode of being, a means of existing and of *causing* to *exist*, that is, a means of causing God who reveals Himself to appear, of "seeing" Him, not to be sure in His essence, but in the form which precisely He reveals by revealing Himself by and to that form ...[29]

In this way, prayer becomes the highest act of the Creative Imagination.[30] Through this the individual begins to tap into the visible manifestations of God to humankind. According to Ibn Arabi, "His [i.e. God's] unknowness" aspires "to be known".[31] Prayer / reflection / meditation then "accomplishes this theophany because in it and through it the 'Form of God' (*surat al-Haqq*) becomes visible to the heart."[32] The eyes then begin to see His Signs as symbols and as reminders of His Beauty.

Theophanic perception is attained in the imagination - *'alam al-mithal'*. Ibn Arabi states that the "Imagination is the organ of theophanic perception ... capable of transmuting sensory data into symbols and external events into symbolic histories."[33] For Rumi, these symbols reveal the spiritual worlds above, where they become transparent and reveal meaning of the beyond, the higher order of reality and finally the Ultimate Reality.[34] Concurring, Ibn Arabi affirms that the imagination "guides ... molds sense perception; that is why it transmutes data into symbols."[35] This way The Hidden One becomes transparent and 'known' to the observer.

In Islamic fine arts, the reliance on naturalism to evoke God's creation serves to highlight the experience of theophany. To appreciate the Beauty of Creation in the Natural world, as presented in Islamic fine arts, the artist attempts to recreate it in various mediums using vibrant colours and variety of floral ensembles. To imitate or recreate the creation according to Ibn Arabi "[...] is essentially the revelation of the Divine Being" and "[...] the creation signifies nothing less than the Manifestation (*zuhur*) of the hidden (*batin*) Divine Being [...]."[36] Such views inspired modern writers, philosophers and scholars.

Henry Corbin cites the nineteenth century German writer and statesman Goethe whose interest in Islam contributed to the publication of work on Sufism. Goethe wrote on literary and aesthetic criticism; and treatises on botany, anatomy, and colour. His immense philosophical interest in Islam and Sufism, and as a scholar, saw the publication of his *Der west-östliche Divan* (*The West-Eastern Divan, The Parliament of East and West*) in 1819. The work represented his homage to the peerless Persian Sufi poet Hafiz (d.1390). Furthermore, in his treatise on the vibrancy of colours used by the artist to stir the soul, Corbin cites Goethe:

The perception of color is an action and reaction of the soul itself which is communicated to the *whole being; an energy* is then emitted through the eyes, a spiritual energy that cannot be weighed or measured quantitatively ... the eye at this point produces another color, *its own color*. The eye searches at the side of a given colored space for a free space where it can produce the color called for by itself.[37]

For colour, according to Goethe "[...] is not a passive impression, but the language of the soul."[38] In the constructed imaginary colourful garden of the mosque aesthetics like the Rustem Pasha Mosque, the observer seeks salvation because the garden of paradise is for "those who have believed and have done good works" (2:25; 4:57), for "those who are God fearing" (3:15; 44:51; 52:17; 78:31), for 'the true servants of God (37:43; 38:49), and for 'those who believe in Our Signs and are submissive' (43:69). However, hope and salvation are not lost on the observer who is questioning his belief for God says in the Qur'an, "Say: O my servants who transgressed against their souls! Despair not of the Mercy of God, for God forgives all sins, for He is Oft-Forgiving and Most Merciful" (39:53). This hope urges the individual to strive to become the ideal human being - *insan al-kamil* as intended by God.

Islamic art leaves to the imagination and the conscience of the observer contemplate on the world to come. The mosque, for example, as a religious space and place of worship enriched with its visual aesthetics are further reminders to the viewer of God's immeasurable Mercy and the hope of an eternal blissful hereafter reflected in the Qur'an. From a Sufi humanist perspective, Sinan's omission of the imagery of Hell[39] allows the viewer in the midst of this temporal paradise to once again enter the state of self-reflection. Rumi writes:

I am the foundation of both reason and ecstasy. Now we realize that the beauty which we saw in forms and fantasies was the reflection of our beauty.[40]

In other words, the beauty one's soul experiences in the 'World of Spirits' reflects the Beauty of God in human form on earth.

Influence of Sufi humanism on Ottoman Renaissance thought and Visual Culture

Sixteenth-century Ottoman Renaissance thought and art are influenced by Sufi humanism of Rumi, Ibn Arabi and the classical ideals of Plato. Influence of Rumi on Ottoman literati is immense. Having lived and preached in Seljuk Konya in the thirteenth century, Rumi's work, the *Mesnevi* (*Mathnawi* in English) a spiritual text of 25,000 verses teaching Sufis how to attain their goal of uniting with God and being truly in love with the Divine. This mystical and esoteric understanding of Islam influenced his contemporaries including Yunus Emre (1238-1320). Others followed in the subsequent centuries including Letafi (d.1582), Nef'i (d.1635) and Ismail Rusuhi (d.1630) are among the followers of Rumi.[41] Furthermore, according to Carl Brockelmann, "… for centuries the Mathnawi [Mesnevi] determined the intellectual outlook of the best elements in the Ottoman Empire," providing its early modern humanist and creative mindsets.[42] In fact, Rumi's *Mesnevi* was among the texts included in the curriculum at Ottoman *madrasas* (theological colleges).[43]

There is historical evidence that suggests Rumi's *Mevlevi* philosophy may have been influenced by the teachings of Ibn Arabi who briefly stayed in Seljuk Konya in 1205 before moving on to Cairo the following year. It is not certain whether the two philosophers met, however, Ibn Arabi's student al-Qunawi later became Rumi's disciple. According to Farrukh, "It was through Qunawi that the intimate doctrines of 'Arabi were conveyed to Rumi […]."[44] Fatih Akçe also confirms that "the mentor of Osman Ghazi [founder of the Ottoman dynasty], Sheikh Edebali (d.1326), received lessons from Ibn Arabi in Damascus" showing deep connection between the Ottomans and the Sufi master.[45] Another scholar from Anatolia followed, Davud-i Kayseri (d.1350) who "[…] gave lectures to others using Ibn Arabi's work."[46] His student Fenari (d.1431) became the first *Şeyhülislam* (the chief theologian) of the Ottoman Empire in Bursa during the reign of Mehmed I.[47] The reverence for Ibn Arabi continued well into the sixteenth century when Selim I, following the conquest of Damascus in 1516 ordered a shrine to be built at the burial place of the Sufi master (*Figure 7*).[48] The two Sufi contemporaries left their mark on early modern Ottoman mysticism, intellectualism and the arts.

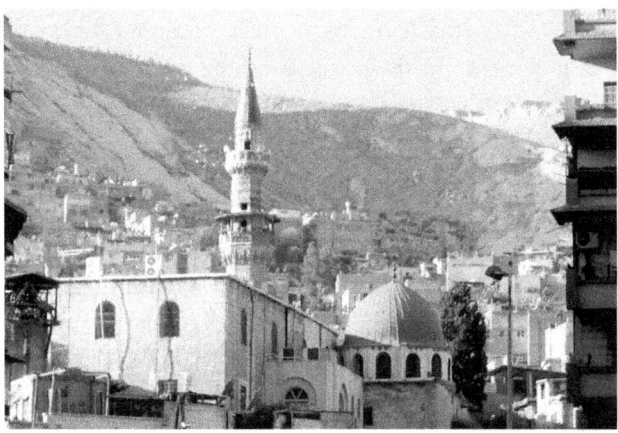

Figure 7. The burial site of Ibn Arabi in Damascus built on the order of Sultan Selim I. Photograph by M. Aksoy, April 2005.

Throughout the Seljuk and Ottoman periods, Sufis contributed to the development of Islamic art. The Mevlana Museum of Konya houses some of the Sufi art works including the earliest manuscript of the *Mesnevi* (1278) and illuminated works from the Seljuk and Ottoman periods. There are numerous Qur'ans inscribed in different calligraphic styles demonstrating the Sufi contributions to the development of this art form throughout the centuries.

Examples of calligraphy shown here [in the museum] include the verses of a ninth century *Kufic* Kor'an inscribed on gazelle-skin parchment, a Kor'an in *thuluth* in Persian dating to the ninth century and various works in different kinds of script, including *reyhani*, *naskhi* (notably the work of the calligrapher Yakut'el-musta'semi), *thuluth-naskhi*, *talik*, *nath-talik*, *divani* and *rik'a*.[49]

The Sufi calligraphers and painters created expressive portrayals using Arabic script for representational drawings, as well as floral designs and personal insignias (*tughras*). On Sufi calligraphy, Frembgen states:

Characterized by the harmony of their lines and the magic of their beauty, many of these works exhibit a special aura: decorating the walls of aesthetically designed rooms in dervish lodges (*khanqah, tekke*), they create not only an important visual dimension in veneration and contemplation of God or charismatic Sufi saints, but also in concrete practices of ritual recollection of God.[50]

The visual expression of Sufi art reinforces the theophanic experience for the observer, drawing him closer to God.

Other Sufi works contributed to the development of Ottoman art. Added to the calligraphic works in the Mevlana Museum, there are: fourteenth century glass lanterns; fifteenth century rugs from the Ushak region of Anatolia with stylised bird-like motifs; silk rugs woven with silver thread containing an image of the Ka'ba framed by bands of *rumis*; musical instruments of the dervishes – the *ney*; and dervish garments including those worn by Rumi himself. These works and others produced are mainly housed in the Sufi lodges (*tekkes*). Sufi lodges are built either adjacent or nearby to public and imperial mosques, including the dervish lodge built next to Rumi's tomb by Süleyman's grandson Murad III in 1584, the Süleymaniye Mosque and Atik Valide Mosque (Mosque of Nurbanu Sultan – 1583, the wife of Selim II).[51] These Sufi art works are a testimony of the influence of Sufism on the development of Ottoman visual culture.

Such works of art housed in the lodges, combined with the ascetic and pious lifestyle of the Sufis complement the Sufi *tasavvuf* philosophy of exemplary behaviour and closeness to God advocated by Rumi and Ibn Arabi. The proximity of the lodges near public and imperial mosques reinforced the Sufi visual culture and its philosophical message. The *tasavvuf* philosophy became ingrained first in Seljuk, then Ottoman spiritual and literary consciousness.

Architecturally, reverence for Rumi and his Sufi order by the Ottoman sultans in the sixteenth century can be seen through the restoration of the master's tomb. The mausoleum of Rumi was built by the Seljuk Emir Süleyman Pervane (d. 1277) in 1274. Later the Ottoman Sultan Bayezid I (d. 1403) commissioned the lobed conical roof with turquoise tiles in 1396 (*Figure 8*).[52] As Mehmet Önder states:

> During the reign of Süleyman the Magnificent, Sinan, the leading architect of the day built a *semahane* [assembly hall for whirling ceremonies] and a *mescid* [chapel] in the complex on imperial orders. The domed dervish cells were surrounding the mausoleum were built during the reign of Murad III [d.1595], on his orders, and the monumental fountain – *şadırvan* – in the courtyard was built during the period of Selim the Grim [d.1520].[53]

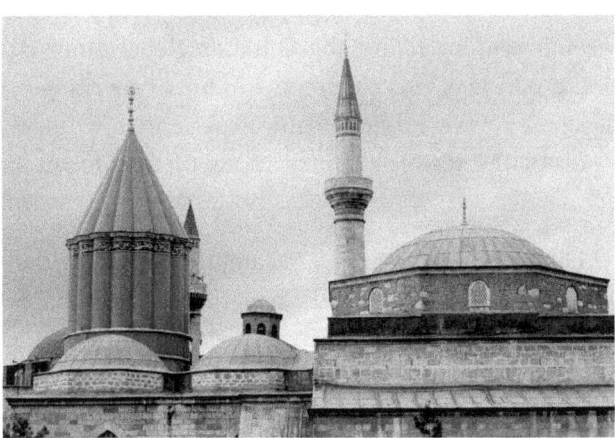

Figure 8. The Mausoleum of Celaleddin Rumi (Mevlana) built by the Seljuks and later restored and expanded by the Ottomans. The fusion of Seljuk and Ottoman aesthetics can be seen in the architecture of the building. Photograph by Metin Mustafa, October 1987.

Such restoration works signified not only reverence for Rumi but also convey the continuity of the royal connection to the great mystic through Mehmed I (d.1421) whose father Bajezid I (d.1403) married Devlet Hatun (d.1414) whose mother Mutahhara Hatun was the granddaughter of Rumi.[54] According to Önder,

> The Ottoman Mevlevi line was later established with the birth of Çelebi Mehmed [i.e. Mehmed I] to Devlet Hatun. Later sultans maintained this hereditary link. Mehmed the Conqueror is known to have had a close relationship with the Mevelevi *pir,* Cemaleddin Çelebi, the son of Pir Adil Çelebi. He was a frequent pilgrim to the tomb of Mevlana, which he restored and granted a number of endowments to the order. His son, Bayezid II bestowed a number of favours on Cemaleddin Çelebi personally, and totally restored Mevlana's, providing it with the ornamentation in its present form.[55]

Sultan Süleyman's continued patronage of Sufi art and mystical rituals in the sixteenth century reflect the Ottoman Renaissance culture and thought of the period. This is expressed in Sinan's writings that invite the observer on a journey of theophanic experience to witness his art as an expression of the visible manifestations of God to humanity and ponder on his salvation.

For Sinan, Ottoman Renaissance art came to represent the Ottoman paradise on earth as a signpost of the next life.[56] He compares his art to "nightingales" inviting all to the "rose garden", the "celestial throne", "Milky Way".[57] Entering a mosque built by Sinan is like entering a "rose garden" whose doors "are like those of Paradise" where the seeker can wash his sins away from the "pool of Kevser, that matchless fountain to be."[58] Like the whirling dervish and the pilgrim circumambulating the Ka'ba during the *hajj* pilgrimage seeking union with God, Sinan, too, affirms that the observer will find salvation, mercy and be absolved of his sins by "Circling the rose garden of the sanctuary ...

Comes there [his mosques] to win God's blessing' and 'free from hell-fire secure."[59]

Influence of Sufism on Islamic art and more specifically the aesthetics of Sinan in the sixteenth century have produced works of art manifesting the spiritual realities (al-haqa'iq) of the Qur'an into earthly expressions through theophanies. Inspired by the Qur'anic revelation, Sufi humanism provided artists like Sinan the philosophical ideology to attain closer relationship with God –tawhid and ittihad through symbols (ta'wil). Furthermore, Sinan's mosque of Rustem Pasha is the embodiment of this early modern Ottoman expression of humanism inspired by Sufism confirming the unique status of Ottoman artistic rhetoric and its distinctive Renaissance narrative.

Like Vasari, the sole purpose of Sinan's works is to promote the arts of the Ottoman world. Sinan's self-aggrandising endorsement reflects the achievements of the Ottomans in the sixteenth century. With their predominantly boastful tone, Sinan's autobiographies promote a lasting legacy in which his works will be the subject of much discussion and admiration. His tendency to boast about his architectural achievements and decorative aesthetics led him to claim that he had created "magnificent" ('azim) works of art by studying and learning from past exemplars. Like Vasari's elevation of Tuscan artists above others, Sinan's boasts work to promote his achievements over that of his contemporaries as well as his predecessors.

Through the works of Sinan, the sixteenth-century understanding of Ottoman notion of rebirth emerges. This understanding expresses a sense of Ottoman historical consciousness and identity in an expanding empire which sees cultural rebirth as part of its self-fashioning and worldview. Sinan's notion of artistic rebirth converges with Vasarian views of rinascita, where stylistic evolution from past exemplars helps shape progress made in the present. This reinforces the Vasarian idea of the Tuscan rinascita as "seeing past events as present."[60] Like their European counterparts, Ottoman artists created new styles (ihtirā sūret) through nezāket (refinement) and, finally, zuhūrat (perfection of the old). By placing the Ottoman voice within the

context of a global Renaissance narrative, this work provides an alternative reading of Sinan's works.

Conclusively, Sufi philosophy is expressed in the Ottoman imperial
architect Sinan's (d.1588) autobiographies that invite the observer on a
journey of theophanic experience to witness his art as an expression of
the visible manifestations of God to humanity and ponder on his salvation. Sinan alludes to the metaphysical nature of his art by comparing
it to the Prophet's ascension (*mi'raj*) to different levels of heaven and
finally meeting God at the "Utmost boundary" (53:14).[61] Witnessing
the Imaginal World of Angels and other spirits by Muhammad,
complement the Qur'anic message of hope of an afterlife. This message
further inspired Muslim artists, including Sinan, to evoke this transcendental experience of the world to come for the observer in their
art. This transcendental experience provides hope and salvation for the
individual seeking *ittihad* through the intercession of the Prophet. In
his autobiographies Sinan states:

> And because that Beloved of God was the cause of all Creation, on
> the Night of the Prophet's miraculous ascent to the Throne of God,
> [that] seal of the seal ring, signet of intercession, and joyful crown
> was exalted and celebrated with the jewelled ornament [...][62]

References to ascension, jewels and ornaments of paradise, and Throne
of God, stimulated the artist's imagination to create works of art to
evoke this Imaginal World. Sinan then continues to allude to his works
in Istanbul 'to be lofty like the heavens' similar to the paradisiacal
wonders experienced by Muhammad.[63] From this viewpoint, the
works of the artist enhances the theophanic experience for the
observer. This mystical element of the Islamic faith went on to inspire
medieval and Renaissance writers, poets and artists including Dante
and Michelangelo. From this perspective, a comparative analysis of
Michelangelo's *Last Judgement* and the Iznik *çini* decorative aesthetics
of the Rustem Pasha Mosque by Sinan are justified. It is within this
overarching framework of the mystical perspective of the transcen-

dental that is articulated in the artworks of the Renaissance masters in Ottoman Istanbul and Italy respectively that forms the basis of the argument in the second half of this book. Before discussing these however, it is significant to explore the technological achievements in Renaissance art: the making of the *buon' fresco* and Iznik *çini*.

PART II

CHAPTER 3

TECHNOLOGY OF
RENAISSANCE ART
BUON' FRESCO AND IZNIK ÇİNİ

The Renaissance epitomised technological advancements not only in the field of engineering seen in the monumental building projects undertaken on both sides of the Mediterranean, but also in the innovative developments in art. These artworks in included Michelangelo's *buon' fresco* of the *Last Judgement* in the Sistine Chapel of the Vatican and the Ottomans' technological breakthrough in tile making or *çini*, producing brilliant vibrant colours in the kilns of Iznik that Sinan utilised in the interior decorative aesthetics of the Rustem Pasha Mosque in Istanbul.

Michelangelo's buon' fresco: The 'Last Judgement'

Michelangelo's *Last Judgement*, a fresco spanning 13.7x12.2 metres and executed on the altar wall of the Sistine Chapel of the Vatican, represents the Divine according to the Christian tradition. At a literal level, the work depicts the Second Coming of Christ and the Final Judgement of all humanity. The souls of people rise and descend to their fates, as judged by Christ, surrounded by prominent saints who have died cruel deaths, including Catherine of Alexandria, Peter, Lawrence, Bartholomew, Paul, Sebastian and John the Baptist. This human representation sharply contrasts with Sinan's reliance on naturalism. The fresco was produced between 1536 and 1541—twenty-five years after Michelangelo finished the Sistine Chapel Ceiling—and took four years to complete.

The *Last Judgement* covers the entire back wall of the Sistine Chapel and is so large that two of Perugino's frescoes had to be destroyed, and two large arched windows walled up, in order to accommodate it. Along with scenes taken largely from the Bible, the master artist also included scenes from classical mythology, such as Cesena as Minos (one of the three judges of the underworld), and at the bottom of the painting the boatman, Charon, from Greek and Roman mythology can be seen ferrying the damned into Hell.[1]

Like Sinan, who did not typically employ the use of Iznik tiles, but did so for the interior of the Rustem Pasha Mosque, Michelangelo was unwilling to create a fresco due to the laboriousness of the task. However, once he had agreed to do so he "prepared for oil paints by lathering on a coating of plaster mixed with resin, a laborious and expensive process."[2] Connor claims that Michelangelo's initial decision to create a fresco in oil was in order to distinguish it from his earlier famous ceiling project, but he did not like the way light reflected off the wall[3] and decided to return to the *buon' fresco* technique. The difficulty in painting the fresco using this technique contributed to the lengthy duration of the project. The challenge in creating a *buon' fresco* was largely related to the proper preparation of the wall; to ensure no cracks would appear after the colours had been applied, as this would destroy the fresco. James A. Connor states, "[f]resco painting requires six layers of underlying plaster, or stucco, all applied with a rule and plummet, to be a reliable surface for the artist."[4] After the six coats had dried and were polished with smooth wood, the colours could be applied. However, despite its laboriousness, an advantage of the *buon' fresco* technique is that the pigments become part of the plaster, and as a result, part of the wall. According to Connor:

The colours applied by the artist would not fade if applied properly, because the moisture evaporated by the lime would leave behind a porous crystalline structure that would in turn absorb the colours and incorporate them into the calcium carbonate that formed as the plaster dried.[5]

This technique ensured that the wall could easily be cleaned and that the colours would not fade, as revealed by the 1999 restoration of the work, where cleaning of the wall unveiled a greater chromatic range than had previously been apparent; orange, green, yellow and blue colours are scattered throughout, stimulating and unifying the complex scene.

The painstaking preparation and conceptualisation of every figure, i.e., their respective positions and their shadows, were vital considerations for Michelangelo. He first created clay models to visualise his images as three-dimensional forms.[6] By holding a candle at various angles near each clay model, Michelangelo studied how light cast shadows on each figure. By moving the candle closer and farther away from the objects he "created different types of light, from sharp, hard light with deep shadows to soft ambient light casting bare, almost ghostly shadows".[7] Michelangelo rejected the richness of the colours he had used on the ceiling, decades earlier, in favour of using only two principal colours. With a combination of greys and browns he created the warm flesh of the naked figures, and combined cobalt blue with azurite for the sky. In order to create a sense of distance and depth, Michelangelo used a light underpaint with almost translucent red.[8] Like the production of Iznik tiles, the Renaissance artist had to understand the properties of each colour and how it might change, either due to the passing of time or, as particularly related to Iznik tiles, due to heat. For Michelangelo, the colours selected had to be earthy to ensure their longevity and be made of calcined travertine, which would produce the richest of whites, called *bianco Sangiovanni*.

Another limitation faced by Michelangelo was that he had to ensure that the plaster was kept moist so that the colours would penetrate. As with the Iznik tile-making process, colour may look one way on wet plaster but an entirely different way once dry. Thus, there is no room for error with either fresco or tile making. In each, if a mistake is made it can only be rectified once the work is dry and able to be corrected by chiselling, and starting again. Such constraints, which were faced by both Michelangelo and Sinan, attest to the determination and dedication of these masters in their pursuit of artistic achievement.

At its inauguration in 1541, the *Last Judgement* received mixed reactions from Michelangelo's contemporaries. One of his students, Condivi, who acknowledged the artist's innovative use of space and technical virtuosity, said:

> In this work Michelangelo expressed all that the art of painting can do with the human figure, leaving out no attitude or gesture whatever.[9]

Similarly, Vasari declared the work as a "great exemplar of the grand manner of painting" where "we are shown the misery of the damned and the joy of the blessed"[10]. However, he also condemned Michelangelo's use of nudity on the figures of Christ and the saints:

> Theatines are the first to say that nudes are not fitting in such a place, showing their parts, even though Michelangelo has exercised tact, in this, and there are scarcely ten in the whole multitude where you can see sexual organs [...] but the very Reverend Cornaro, who went to study them for a long time, seems to have it right, saying that if Michelangelo were willing to give him in a picture just one of these figures, he would gladly pay him whatever he asked, and I agree, because I do not believe one can see the likes of it anywhere else.[11]

The unease felt by many of the fresco's viewers was evident, with the appreciation of its aesthetic qualities overshadowed by critics such as Pietro Aretino, a writer of pornography,[12] who in his letter of 1545 deplored the indecency of the images—"in the greatest temple built to God, in the most sacred chapel upon the earth."[13] According to John O'Malley, because the Calvinist and Catholic influences in Europe at the time had such "an impact on the appreciation of art"[14], while the fresco was not destroyed the private parts of Christ and the saints were painted over. Unfortunately, the work's contemporary critics failed to appreciate that, as Hammer states, "Michelangelo was offering a new interpretation of the Last Day" as an expression of "spiritual rebirth" and the "transitional period from Renaissance Humanism to the developments of the Catholic Counter-Reformation."[15]

Sinan's Iznik çini: The Mosque of Rustem Pasha

Like Michelangelo's grandiose fresco, the unique Mosque of Rustem Pasha, Istanbul, which was designed and built by Sinan in the name of Sultan Süleyman's Grand Vizier—who twice served the Sultan in the highest office of the Empire during 1544-1553 and 1555-1561. The mosque was the first major decorative Iznik tile project to be undertaken in Ottoman history. It is, therefore, worthy of analysis and comparison to other great contemporary Renaissance works. Despite this fact, no major scholarly attention has been paid to the interior of the Mosque of Rustem Pasha since 1971, when Walter B. Denny's, *The Ceramics of the Mosque of Rustem Pasha and the Environment of Change*,[16] identified the tiles, motifs, designs and technical aspects of Iznik craftsmanship. Denny focused on the production method of the tiles and an anagogical reading of the motifs with respect to the Qur'an's allusions to Paradise. However, Denny's analysis lacks a didactic interpretation that intertwines with an anagogical reading of the tiles, and therefore, ignores any self-examination or reflection that Sinan would have had of his work. The careful planning and placement of the tile panels, with specific designs and motifs in precise locations inside the mosque, allow for a much deeper eschatological reading. Subsequent research, such as work by Michael D. Willis (1987) and Fatih Cimok (2001), are also largely reliant on Denny's interpretation.

While it is beyond the scope of this dissertation to examine every wall panel of the mosque, a close analysis of the entrance panel, i.e., the *qibla* wall and the *mihrab*, demonstrates an Ottoman representation of the Divine and salvation, through Sinan's unique use of Iznik tiles.

Unfortunately, it is not known whether the mosque was completed before Sinan's death in 1561—as many foundation inscriptions on the monument are absent. However, the inauguration of the Rustem Pasha Mosque occurred 20 years after the unveiling of Michelangelo's *Last Judgement*. According to Willis, "[a]dditional information is provided by the panoramic view of Istanbul prepared by Melchior Lorichs in 1559 suggests that the complex was completed. This drawing shows the Rustem Pasha Mosque near the Odun Kapısı, between the great mosques of Süleyman and Beyazit."[17] Melchior Lorichs's (d. 1564) panorama of Constantinople (1559) indicates that the structure of the mosque must have been completed by 1559 and that the tile revetments were in place by 1561, but the details of the mosque could not have been finalised until Sinan drew up the plans and the building supervisor, Mehmet Bey, received instructions from Princess Mihrimah (the pasha's widow and Süleyman's daughter). According to Necipoğlu, the final product of the Rustem Pasha Mosque was made possible through the combined deliberations of the trio.[18] This assertion, however, is incorrect because Sinan never repeated this ostentatious tiling in any other of his mosque interiors. Like Michelangelo, he was deterred by the laborious nature of decorating the interior of a building with thousands of tiles, where each tile was intricately connected to form a unified visual narrative based on floral naturalism.

In the early seventeenth century, one of Sinan's successors and pupils, Kasım Agha, followed in the great architect's tradition by building a mosque for the Valide Mahpeyker Sultan. Agha decorated its interior with Kutahya tiles, which were sourced from a central Anatolian town that took over tile production after the decline of Iznik. Therefore, the final decision to cover virtually every vertical interior surface of the Rustem Pasha Mosque with tiles, including both sides of the galleries, was likely that of Mihrimah Sultan. This view has also been supported by historians from the period, such as Ramazanzade Mehmed (c.1562-65) and Hasanbeyzade (1595-1635), who praised Mihrimah Sultan for building such a mosque for her husband's soul. As Ramazanzade states:

> Her Highness the Sultana's pious deed on behalf of the late Rustem Pasha's soul: She built such a luminous Friday mosque, that those who saw it think it was made of light [...] resembling paradise. Ever since the azure dome of the moon and the sun (an allusion to the princess's name) no such ornamented and pleasant-looking building has ever been erected, designed, or founded on the surface of the earth and under the heavens.[19]

The historian Hasanbeyzade concurs with Ramazanzade, attributing the building of the mosque to the pasha's wife, "[f]or her husband Rustem Pasha's soul she built in Tahtakale an artistic and elegant Friday mosque".[20] As the executor of her husband's will, Mihrimah Sultan did not spare any expense in providing her husband's soul with a beautiful mosque. Similarly, in Rustem Pasha's own *vakfiye* document there is acclaim for his wife for her contributions.[21] From such documents it is evident that the project was a husband-wife venture that Sinan had to accommodate for in his planning and decoration of the mosque.

The Rustem Pasha Mosque is celebrated as a Sinan masterpiece and is one of Rustem Pasha's posthumous legacies, and no other mosque displays the same levels of beauty or variety of Iznik tiles. The tile designs are directly inspired by textile patterns to which the pasha's own silk loom industry workers must have contributed. Additionally, the influence of textile patterns on Iznik designs is evident in the caftan motifs of the sultans from the fifteenth century, which are housed at the Topkapi Palace Museum. According to Denny, the mosque served as the site of a design competition for both Istanbul designers and Iznik tile manufacturers. According to Denny:

In the variety of designs, in which at least a dozen artists must have had a role, we can see a summary of the past half-century of Ottoman art and the harbingers of the creativity of the next-half century. There are cautious innovations and conservative repetitions of old themes; there are artistic successes and failure; there are masterpieces and journeyman efforts. Taken together, the decorations of Rustem Pasha's mosque constitute a stunning proclamation of the state of the arts in the Ottoman Empire in 1561, the year of Rustem Pasha's death.[22]

The mosque interior represents the ostentatious zenith of centuries of evolution of tile and ceramic art, beginning in the Bursa mosques and culminating in the short-lived renaissance of Iznik tiles in the imperial mosques of sixteenth-century Istanbul. The perfection of the Iznik tile-work conveys the development of this art form and represents a moment of artistic change in the development of Turkish ceramics, and an evolution of the classical Ottoman-Turkish style. As Fatih Cimok notes:

Their lavish employment in this monument may show that Sinan, Sultan Süleyman's chief architect who built the mosque, had not yet decided to use this new medium in architecture. In his other monuments, he appeared to use underglaze polychrome tiles more economically. The unusual number of motifs encountered in the mosque also point out that neither the decorators nor the architect had decided what designs to favor.[23]

The tiles used in the mosque, and during the sixteenth century indicate technical and aesthetic prowess, which according to Kuban "rival[s] any of the ceramic styles in the history of art"[24] and represent "Turkish art *par excellence*".[25] In fact, Denny describes the mosque as a "theatre for the drama of Iznik tiles"[26], but equally, it could be considered a museum of Ottoman 'tile frescoes' that mesmerise the eyes and give believers hope in an afterlife.

Like the laborious preparation of Michelangelo's fresco above, Sinan too had to endure much painstakingly frustrating moments and planning to put the art of Iznik into practice. Isil Akbaygil has shown that 85% of the material in Iznik tiles was made of ground quartz, a substance unlike any other, that gave the tiles their lasting lustre and would allowed them to retain colour for many centuries: "[t]hat's what makes the colours so good and bright as well as durable."[27] The Iznik Foundation described how the quartz was mixed with earth or sand and clay into a mouldable compound. John Covel, the Chaplain to the Levant Company who visited Iznik in 1677, noted the sand mixture used by Ottoman artisans at the kilns. [28] However, Julian Raby believes that even during the decline of Iznik in the mid-seventeenth century, potters would have used quartz-silica instead of sand, as indicated by a chemical analysis of pottery fragments. His findings indicate a composition of 85% quartz, 10% white clay and 5% glass frit.[29]

Once Iznik potters had placed the formed clay and quartz compound into a frame and left it to dry for 20 days, the dried product was ground to a perfectly smooth surface, sized, and each tile individually cut. In most ceramic art the next step would typically involve painting and decorating the tiles, applying a protective glaze and then firing in a kiln. However, as revealed by Akbaygil, the Iznik process was unique; after grinding and smoothing the surface of the tiles, potters poured a liquefied thin quartz glaze over each tile, and then fired them in a kiln, which gave the tiles the vibrancy that became synonymous with Iznik work. Another aspect of this process that was unique to Iznik tiles is that they were baked, twice, at 900 degrees Celsius and with a double glaze. Between pulverising, moulding, drying and baking the tiles, the Iznik Foundation calculated that it took six weeks to produce a batch of tiles, not including any time needed for decorating, which was considered to be the most painstaking part. The Iznik Foundation has found that including the design process, a total of ten weeks were needed to produce a complete Iznik tile.

After the tiles had been baked, the decorating process consisted of applying black ink contour lines that would later contain the coloured pigments. As Julian Raby states—a "stencil is laid over the tile or vessel and charcoal dust sprinkled over the pricking, so that the design is pounced on to the pottery."[30] There is some debate over whether Iznik artists also used stencils for their designs. However, there is evidence to support that this was the case, specifically found in *firmans* (Ottoman edicts), which refer to the Sultan's Court sending stencil *numune* (samples) to Iznik. As Raby notes, there is "unequivocal evidence that the Court sent designs to Iznik, at least for tiles: an unpublished *firman* of *Rebiyulevvel* 1013/1604 September, relating to tiles for the tomb which was about to be built for the late Sultan Mehmed III, mentions the designs (*resimler*) for the tiles of the tomb of Sultan Murad III who died in 1595."[31]

Colouring the tiles was laborious and a specialised skill. Each Ottoman artist working at the Iznik ateliers, like today's artists working at the Iznik Foundation, specialised in their own colour due to the different densities of colours. In another process that was unique to Iznik tiles, once the tile decoration had been completed, the tile was covered with quartz glaze for a final baking session in the kiln and this produced the, now famous, vibrant Iznik colours. For the potters, the "most important Iznik colour was blue, which was produced from cobalt oxide", and "they combined cobalt oxide and copper oxide in the glaze."[32] Such processes are what make Iznik colours unique. However, between the painting process and turning out of the final product, the artists and potters sometimes found that the final colour was not as expected. For example, the colour red used during the decorating process may have turned into turquoise blue during the baking process, while light pink may have become red. This, as well as the overall painstakingness of the production process, perhaps explains why Sinan did not repeat his use of this medium in any other work.

The tiles of the Rustem Pasha Mosque are characterised by their stark white background, against which the vibrant colours are brilliantly offset. Since matte, opaque tones were not suitable for architectural decoration because they needed to make a visual impact with the observer signifying the patron's power and prestige, Ottoman artists sought new decorative media that employed brilliant glazes and sharp clear colours over such a background. As Julian Raby explains: "[t]he brilliance of these colours was not, of course, visible to the [tiler ...] as he painted. It was the heat of the furnace which transmuted them from a sludge to grey to a brilliant hue. The [tiler ...] had, therefore, to imagine the polychrome effect as he painted."[33] Additionally, Kingery and Vandiver have shown that red is perhaps the most difficult of underglaze colours to attain during the baking process[34], and therefore, would have led it to become the most highly sought after. When Iznik potters were able to achieve the colour red in around the 1550s, using Armenian bole, which they called *kil-i ermeni*, the coral colour effect it created was unmatched by any other ceramic tradition.[35]

Due to the collective nature of Ottoman authorship and its oral culture, the Iznik craftsmen did not leave any writings behind, nor are their names known to us today. This situation has contributed to Iznik craftsmen's technological achievements being unrecognised as a Renaissance accomplishment. However, the technological accomplishments of these Ottoman artists equal those of the Renaissance artists, particularly in relation to perspective and proportion. Furthermore, it is noteworthy to reiterate that the laborious nature of the respective works of Michelangelo and Sinan are attributed to the technological advancements to produce a *buon' fresco* and Iznik *çini*. These two art forms are integral in the art repertoire that underpin and celebrate the Mediterranean *zeitgeist* without which the arts of the Renaissance in the Mediterranean basin would not make sense.

CHAPTER 4

MICHELANGELO AND SINAN

BETWEEN PROPHET MUHAMMAD'S 'MIR'AJ' AND DANTE'S 'DIVINE COMEDY'

Theological interpretations of Christianity and Islam respectively influenced the art of Michelangelo and Sinan. Both Christian and Islamic eschatology advocate the ascension of the body after death to face judgement and attain salvation in the afterlife. This religious philosophy is reflected in the scriptures of the New Testament and the Qur'an respectively. St. Paul, *Letter to the Corinthians* 2, xii, 1-4 writes: "I know a man in Christ who – whether in his body or out of his body, I cannot say, God alone knows – was plucked up to the third heaven... and heard inexpressible words..." Similarly, the Qur'anic verse (53:1-10) affirms:

For the star, when it goes down! Your companion does not wander, is not deceived, and does not speak his impulse. No, because it is revelation revealed, taught to him by a power of forces, wise, balancing itself high on the sublime horizon! Then it came down... came close... and revealed to his servant that which it revealed...[1]

The Qur'anic verse describes Prophet Muhammad's Night Journey (*Isra*) and his *Mir'aj* (ascension to heaven). The Night Journey from Mecca to Jerusalem is also mentioned in the Qur'an (17:1): "Allah said: Praise be to Allah Who enabled His slave, Muhammad, to make the journey at night from *Masjid al-Haram* in Makkah to *Masjid al-Aqsa* in Jerusalem, which is surrounded by a blessed land." The Prophet took this night journey from Mecca to Jerusalem on a creature named Buraq, with a human face and the body of a mule. According to Bukhari (d. 870), one of the collectors of the *hadiths* (collections of the sayings of Muhammad that are not included in the Qur'an), "Then he [Gabriel] brought the Buraq, handsome-faced and bridled, a tall, white beast, bigger than the donkey but smaller than the mule."[2] He then, with Gabriel ascended to the different levels of the heavens where he met the prophets Adam, Idris, Jesus, John the Baptist, Joseph, Aaron, Moses, and Abraham. The Prophet ascended to the Seven Heavens on stairs, called *al-mirqat*, in which one step is made of gold and the next of silver, and so on. According to the narrative, from Mecca, Muhammad and Gabriel sped northwards beyond Yathrib (Medina) and beyond Khaybar reaching Jerusalem in the same night. Reaching the temple [the Rock] at Jerusalem,[3] Muhammad was met by a company of other biblical Prophets at the holy site. Ibn Ishaq (704-768), one of the earliest biographers of Muhammad continues the narrative from al-Hasan:

> The apostle and Gabriel went their way until they arrived at the temple in Jerusalem. There he found Abraham, Moses, and Jesus among a company of prophets. The apostle acted as their imam in prayer.[4]

Muhammad then ascends further to the next heaven with Gabriel, reaching "[...] the Lote Tree of the utmost boundary" (53: 14). Here, Muhammad prostrates before the Light of God and is shown the inhabitants and the worlds of paradise and hell (*Figures 9a-i*).[5]

One of the earliest poems and illustrations of the *Isra* and *Mir'aj* comes from Tabriz miniature paintings c.1360-70, a portion of which is housed in various museums including the Bibliotheque Nationale in Paris, Topkapı Palace Museum in Istanbul and British Museum, Figures 9a-b. Mir-Heidar's 1436-37 *Miraj Nameh* production from Herat (Afghanistan) is another version of the story illustrated and accompanied with eastern Turkish text commissioned by Timur's son, Shahrukh seen in Figures 9c-g.[6] By the sixteenth century both the Safavid and Ottoman artists were producing their own versions of the spiritual narrative depicted in Figures 9h and 9i.

The seventh century story of Prophet Muhammad's *Isra* and *Mi'raj* inspired Islamic theologians, poets, philosophers and artists for centuries. This concept of the afterlife and the world to come dominated the religious artworks in the Muslim East. Inspired by the Qur'anic Surah 17:1 and the *hadiths* of the story of the *mi'raj*, between the fourteenth and sixteenth centuries, Timurid, Persian and Ottoman painters from Tabriz, Herat and Istanbul produced works to illustrate this spiritual event of the afterlife in the *Mi'raj-name* (The Night Journey and Ascension of the Prophet) seen in Figures 9a-i.[7] In Figure 9b, Prophet Muhammad with Gabriel stand before the gate of Paradise guarded by the Angel Ridwan. In Figures 9c-d and 9h, Mir Heidar and the sixteenth century Tabriz miniaturist Sultan Muhammad, depict Paradise against a turquoise background with fruit trees, animals, flowing rivers and blooming floral ensembles, winged angels and other heavenly creatures, *houris*, as mentioned in the Qur'an (44: 54, 52:20, 55:72). In contrast, the Timurid artist in Figures 9e and 9f captures the darkness lit up with the burning fire during the visit to Hell by Muhammad and Gabriel. Figure 9f portrays the punishment of the evildoers who squander the inheritance of orphans with the red demons pouring a poisonous brew down the throats of the damned. The climactic point of the spiritual journey of Prophet Muhammad, however, is meeting God and submitting to His will before His Throne. Mir Heidar represents this most significant moment by portraying Muhammad enveloped by the Light of God at the final destination beyond the empyrean domain seen in Figure 9g. Venturing beyond the "Lotus of the Utmost Boundary near it is the Garden of Abode" the

veil is lifted for Muhammad.[8] At this point where human will and
God's will unite as one, Muhammad prostrates and stands before his
Lord, and becomes a witness to His Signs. In the presence of the Holy
of Holies, Mir Heidar represents Prophet Muhammad entirely
enveloped in the golden flame that emanate from his body. The flame
supports him as he prostrates before His Lord at the Utmost Boundary
against the background of blue and gold sky.

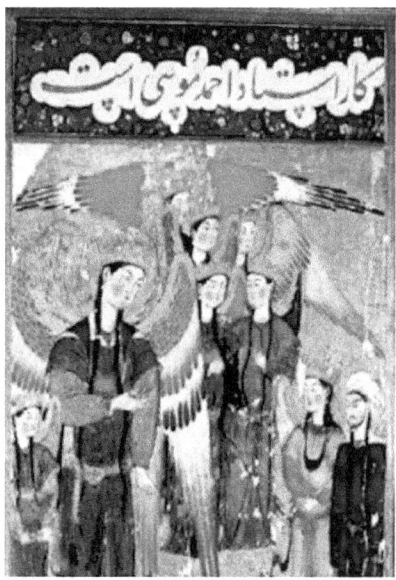 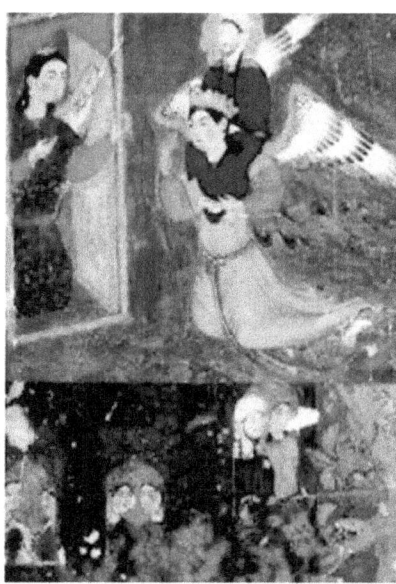

*Figures 9a, 9b. Left, Muhammad (far right) and the Archangel Gabriel
standing in front of a giant angel. From the Mi'raj-name, Tabriz (1360-70).
Right, Muhammad on Gabriel's shoulders arriving at the gate of Paradise
guarded by Angel Ridwan. From the Mi'raj-name, Tabriz (1360-70), Topkapı
Palace, Istanbul. Photograph reproductions.*

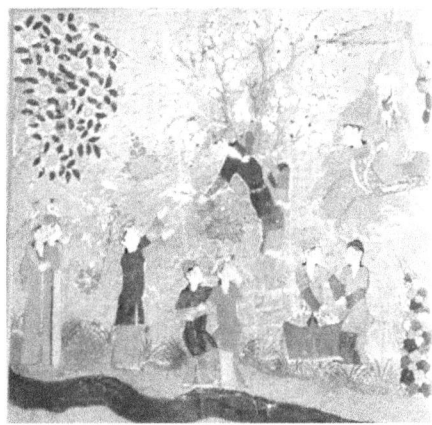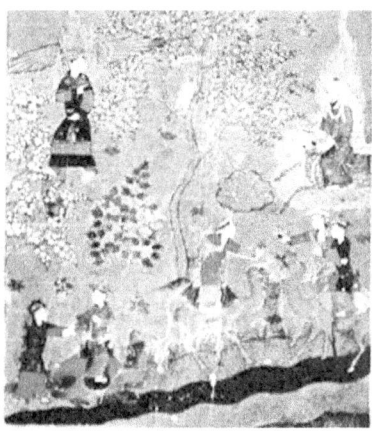

Figures 9c, 9d. Muhammad's visit to Paradise with Buraq and Archangel Gabriel, 15th century Timurid depictions by Mir Heidar from Herat school of painting (Afghanistan), c.1436. Bibliotheque Nationale, Paris. Photograph reproductions.

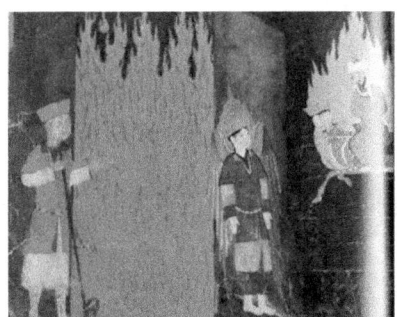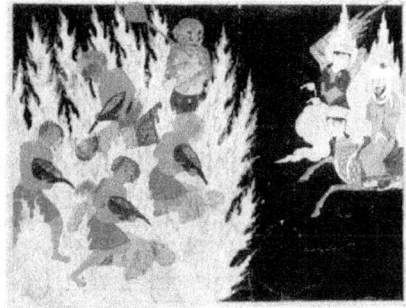

Figures 9e, 9f. Left, Muhammad at the gate of Hell guarded by the angel Malik; right, Muhammad visiting the sinners who squander the inheritance of orphans in Hell with Gabriel, 15th century Timurid depictions by Mir Heidar from Herat school of painting (Afghanistan), c.1436. Bibliotheque Nationale, Paris. Photograph reproductions.

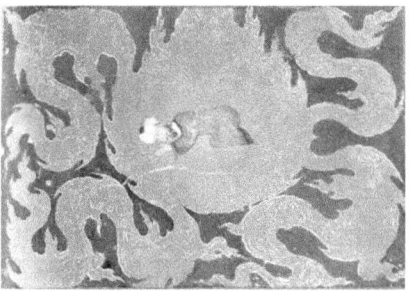

Figure 9g. Muhammad enveloped by the Light of God bows down to worship the Eternal at the Utmost Boundary. Painting by Mir Heidar, Timurid Herat (Afghanistan), c.1436. Bibliotheque Nationale, Paris. Photograph reproduction.

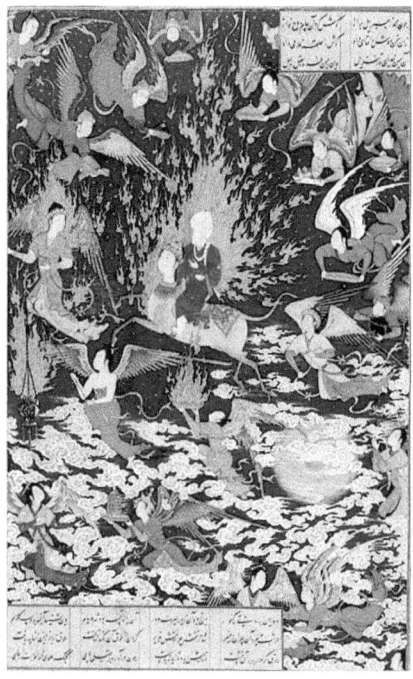

Figure 9h. Ascent of Muhammad to Heaven (ca. 1539–1543), ascribed to Tabriz miniaturist Sultan Muhammad, from the Khamseh of Nizami, Safavid Iran. British Library. Photograph reproduction.

The Prophet's night journey also inspired Ottoman poets. One of the earliest Ottoman epic poems, the *Mevlid-i Şerif*, about the life of Prophet Muhammad was composed by the Sufi Süleyman Çelebi in c.1409. It became widely known throughout the Ottoman realms during Sinan's lifetime and was recited during a festival "which Murad III instituted in A.H. 996 (1589) in honour of the birthday of the Prophet" and one that continues to this day.[9] Çelebi describes the Prophet's *mi'raj* experience in the following words:

That night the Prophet roamed, led on by passion, To view the spheres with comprehending glances ... From each he garnered store of hidden wisdom ... [until] He saw and crossed those empyrean spaces, / And stood at last before the Lord Almighty. / There, Majesty revealed to the Beloved In fullest light, aspects of His Beauty. He saw the Lord of Glory full and clearly / As will his followers in the World Hereafter.[10]

The recital of the epic poem becoming an integral part of the early modern Ottoman cultural and religious practices added weight to the production of an Ottoman illustrated manuscript of the Prophet's life. In the latter part of the sixteenth century, Sultan Murad III commissioned an Ottoman version of the *Siyer-i Nebi* (Life of Prophet Muhammad, c.1594-95), depicting scenes from the Prophet's journey to heaven seen in Figure 9i.[11] The availability of the fourteenth century Tabriz illustrations and others like it, including Figures 9a-e at the Topkapı Palace suggests Sinan may have had access to them for inspiration.

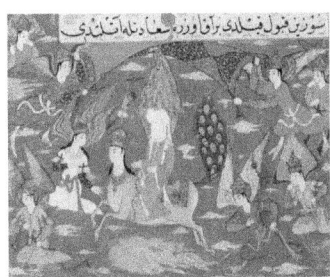

Figure 9i. Prophet Muhammad riding Buraq to Paradise, Ottoman depiction in Siyer –i Nebi, c.1594-95, Topkapı Palace, Istanbul. Photograph reproduction.

It was inevitable that such fantastical narratives deeply entrenched in the consciousness of various Islamic civilisations including that of the early modern Ottomans would inspire artists like Sinan to represent Paradise through naturalistic elements that became synonymous with Iznik *çini* (tile).

Another Islamic figure believed to have influenced Dante is the great Andalusian Sufi, Ibn Arabi (1165-1240).[12] The story of the *mi'raj* came to represent a personal and mystical search for meaning for Ibn Arabi. He wrote about his own personal *mi'raj* experience in the *Al-Futuhat al-Makkiyya* ("The Meccan Revelations") written between 1203 and 1240 following his *hajj* pilgrimage to Mecca in 1202. At the heart of Ibn Arabi's discussion is humanity's "divine vision" (*ru'ya*) to attain union with God (*Ittihad*) by reaching "stages" or "stations" of personal ascension.[13] However, to attain this union is not easy. He refers to himself as *salik* to emphasise the difficulty of achieving oneness with God: "Even now [i.e., after reaching the highest spiritual station) I am still voyaging."[14] In his analysis of Ibn Arabi's metaphysical journey, Carlo Saccone writes:

[The] protagonists are a theologian and a philosopher, the one the perfect type who accepts faithfully the dictates of Revelation, and the other of whom entrusts himself exclusively to the light of human reason. The stages prior to the ascent through the heavens symbolise for Ibn 'Arabi the journey towards natural perfection obtained by the two with the correction of passions and the mortification of the instincts ... At this point, Ibn 'Arabi suggests, theology and philosophy coincide perfectly, since both reason and faith lead to the same result: liberation from the human passions. The two of them begin their celestial ascent. The philosopher uses the famous Buraq, who is here the symbol of human reason in its "speculative" use, as Dante would say, while the theologian uses the famous light-filled garland, the sign of divine Grace.[15]

Similarly, Dante in *Convivio* speaks of "practical use" of the intellect like Ibn Arabi where the practical and lower intellect, he calls the *ingegno.*[16] Dante's narrative in the *Divine Comedy* shares similarities with Prophet Muhammad and Ibn Arabi's ascension to heaven.

Influence of the story of the Mi'raj on Dantean thought

Like Islam, Christianity also continued in its mystical development since the Middle Ages. Throughout the development of the history of Christianity, the Church preoccupied itself with the nature of the Divine, paths to salvation and attaining eternal life. These ideas came to dominate Christian dogma and entered the visual vocabulary of Christianity. Furthermore, coming into contact with the burgeoning Islamic civilisation since the seventh century, through military conflict, trade and cultural exchanges along geographic borders, Christianity increasingly became influenced by its cultural other. As Jung explains:

> This [i.e. mystical] development is important because ... it symbolized the tendency to remove the centre of man and his faith from the earth and to "elevate" it into the spiritual sphere. This tendency sprang from the desire into action Christ's saying: "My kingdom is not of this world." Earthly life, the world, and the body were therefore forces that had to be overcome. Medieval man's hopes were thus directed to the beyond, for it was only from paradise that the promise of fulfilment beckoned.[17]

Historically speaking, the influence of Islamic thought on Christianity has been well documented.[18] From Albertus Magnus (d. 1280) to Thomas Aquinas (d. 1274), Islamic thought had a profound influence on the development of Christian theology. Renan, in his work *Averroes and Averroism*, did not hesitate to affirm that the saintly master of St. Thomas Aquinas owed everything to Averroes.[19] Like Islamic intellectual thought, spiritual and eschatological understandings also contributed to the literary development of Europe. The *hadiths* of the story of the night journey and Ibn Arabi's *Kitab al-isra' ila maqam al-asra* (Book of the Night Journey Towards the Majesty of the [Most] Generous) had been translated first into Spanish then later into Latin and

French around 1264 as *Liber Scalae Machometi* (The Book of Muhammad's Ladder) and *Livre de l'Eschiele Mahomet*. Alfonso X of Castille commissioned the Spanish version. The circulation of the legend had reached Europe and Italy after 1264.[20] This has significant similarities to Dante's *Paradiso* the spheres of paradise. The closest one gets to Dante, is mentioned by Saccone:

A straight quotation of the *Libro della Scala* was found in the encyclopaedic poem *Il Dittamondo* (Book V, Canto xii, vv. 82-102; Canto xiii, vv. 25-42), written between 1350 and 1360 by Fazio degli Uberti, a Tuscan poet from the generation following Dante's and nephew of the famous Farinata; a second appearance related to the Dominican missionary Riccoldo da Montecroce, who went to Baghdad at the end of the thirteenth century and returned to Florence in 1301; he inserts a long section of the legend into one of his polemical works, *Contra legem Saracenorum*.[21]

Saccone informs that various versions of the story circulated in Europe that "bore witness to the widest distribution in Italy and in Europe of knowledge related to the Muhammadan *mi'raj*."[22]

A similar story of the ascension of the souls into paradise or hell is also seen in the *Divine Comedy* of Dante (1265-1321), whose works Michelangelo and other artists including Giovanni di Paolo (1403-1482) and Botticelli (1445-1510) knew well.[23] Dante's imaginative work of the afterlife inspired the Renaissance artists like the *mi'raj* story of Prophet Muhammad inspired Muslim artists in the fifteenth and sixteenth centuries. As the story of the *mi'raj* was circulating in Italy at the time, like the *Mi'raj-name* (Book of the *Mi'raj*) manuscript of the Muslim artists, Giovanni di Paolo's illuminations depict Dante's journey to Purgatory, Hell and Paradise with Beatrice (*Figure 10a*). According to Benjamin David, "[…] the painter Giovanni di Paolo illustrate much of the complexity of the ambivalence of Dante's own representations of the body in *Paradiso*" where "[…] the souls appear as golden-haired naked bodies in groups" as seen in Figure 10c.[24]

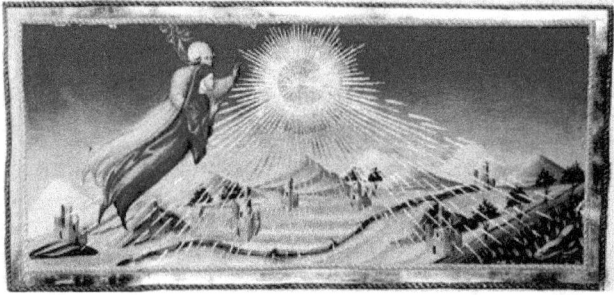

Figure 10a. The Ascension of Dante and Beatrice. Giovanni di Paolo, c.1444-1452. British Library. Photograph reproduction.

The familiarity with the Islamic narrative of Muhammad's ascension to Paradise makes it more likely to ascertain the belief that Dante had access to the *Isra* and *Mir'aj* stories. Like Muhammad ascending beyond the physical existence meeting God at the Abode of Peace, so too, Dante, similarly, travels beyond the empyrean where he is transformed to be more beautiful than ever before at the Light of God. Here, at the throne of God, Dante, like Muhammad, becomes enveloped in light allowing him to see God and experience Divine Love.[25] In Canto XXX, Dante states,

> *Like sudden lightning scattering the spirits*
> *of sight so that the eye is then too weak*
> *to act on other things it would perceive,*
>
> *such was the living light encircling me,*
> *leaving me so enveloped by its veil*
> *of radiance that I could see no thing.*
>
> *The Love that calms this heaven always welcomes*
> *into Itself with such a salutation,*
> *to make the candle ready for its flame.*[26]

Unlike Muhammad's experience at the Throne of God where the Almighty is indescribable and indiscernible, in Dante's version, he sees three equally large circles occupying the same space, representing the

Holy Trinity, the Father, the Son, and the Holy Spirit. By anthropomorphising God, it is within these three circles that Dante discerns the
human form of Christ (*Figures 10b-c*).[27] By altering the narrative to suit
the Christian doctrine of the Trinity, the inclination for later artists
during the Renaissance to use Dante as inspiration for their works of
religious art becomes clear.

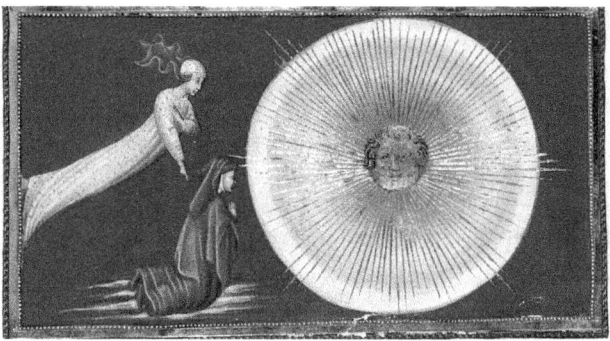

*Figure 10b. Dante and Beatrice seeing three large circles occupying the same
space, representing the Holy Trinity. Giovanni di Paolo, c.1444-1452. British
Library. Photograph reproductions.*

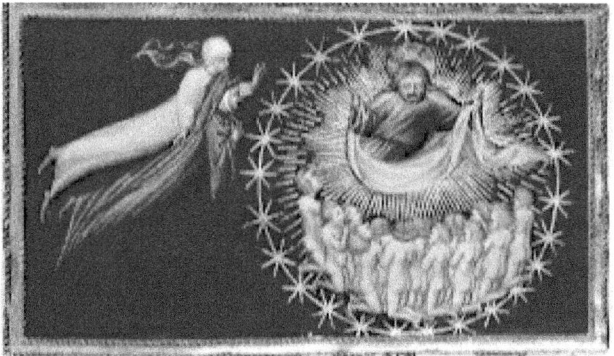

*Figure 10c. Dante and Beatrice witnessing Christ's triumph looking down on
group of kneeling souls enclosed in a circle of stars. Giovanni di Paolo, c.1444-
1452. British Library. Photograph reproduction.*

Similarly, in Botticelli's painting, *Chart of Hell* (c.1480-1495), also inspired by Dante, the description of Hell is visualised through the nine circles where souls are tortured for eternity echoing Muhammad's journey to Hell witnessing the tormented souls of the sinners and demons above (*Figures 10d-e*). Interestingly, his 1481 illustration 'Sowers of Discord' depicts Dante's ninth circle of Hell where the artist places Muhammad there for all eternity along with the Roman poet Virgil and Judas Iscariot (*Figure 10f*). Karen Armstrong sums up this act in the following words:

[...] because Muslim accounts of the *miraj*, Muhammad's ascent to heaven, affected Dante's account of his imaginative journey through hell, purgatory and heaven in The Divine Comedy, even though with typical Western schizophrenia ... he put the Prophet himself in one of the lowest circles of hell.[28]

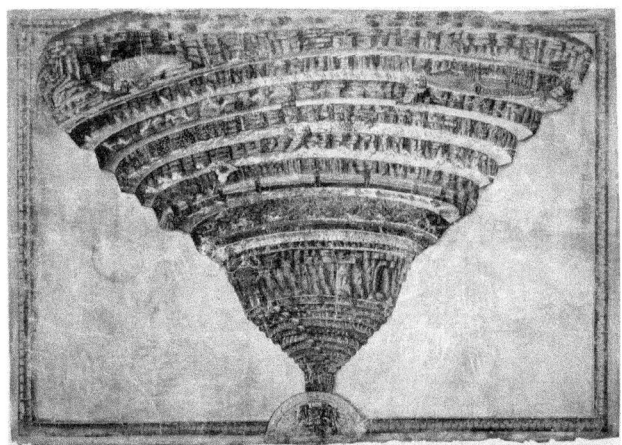

Figure 10d. Botticelli's painting 'Chart of Hell' (c.1480-1495) inspired by Dante's Inferno in Divine Comedy representing the nine circles of Hell where souls are tortured for eternity. Photograph reproduction.

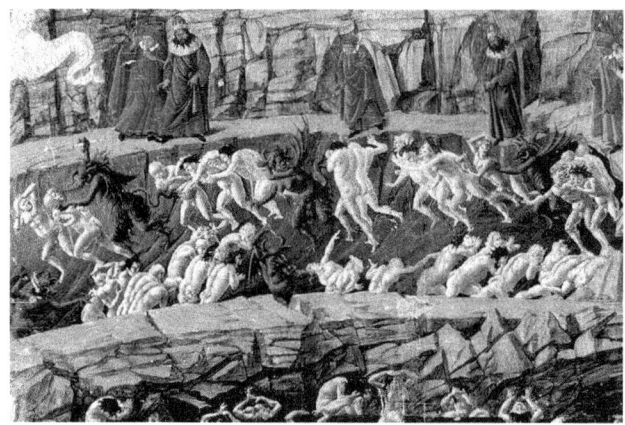

Figure 10e. Detail, the Eighth Circle of Hell from Botticelli's 'Chart of Hell' (c.1480-1495) resided by the fraudulent sinners. Photograph reproduction.

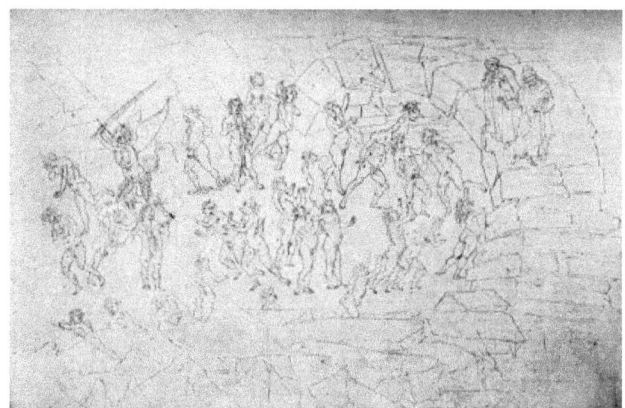

Figure 10f. Botticelli's 1481 illustration, 'Sowers of Discord' is of one of the earliest printed editions of Dante's Inferno also depicting Muhammad as one of the protagonists in Hell. Photograph reproduction.

The similarities between the *mi'raj* of Prophet Muhammad and Dante's *Divine Comedy* require some consideration before analysing the works of Michelangelo and Sinan. There is historical evidence to also suggest that the Florentine poet Dante may also have been influenced by medieval Islamic thought of the Andalusian Sufi mystic Ibn Arabi and the story of his own *Mir'aj*.[29] In 1926, a Spanish scholar and a Catholic priest, Miguel Asin Palacios published *Escatología musulmana en la Divina Comedia* (*Islamic Eschatology in the Divine Comedy*).[30] In this work, Palacios describes the analogies between medieval Islamic philosophy and the *Divine Comedy*. He argued that Dante imitated many features of and episodes about the hereafter from the spiritual writings of Ibn Arabi of the "Imaginal World" (*mithal*) and "World of Souls and Lights" (*malakut*), and from Prophet Muhammad's *Isra* and *Mir'aj* to heaven.[31] Palacios in the *Escatología* argues the "allegorical-mystical adaptations" and the "literary imitations" of the story.[32] Palacios writes of his interest in the matter:

> I ventured to call the attention of specialists to the close resemblance that found between the general outlines of the ascension of Dante and Beatrice throughout the spheres of Paradise, and another allegory of the ascension and a philosopher, in the *Futuhat*, written by the great Sufi of Murcia, Ibn Arabi ... The question so raised was of interest: for if not merely the neo-Platonic metaphysics of ... Ibn Arabi, but the allegorical form in which the latter [Ibn Arabi] cast his Ascension may have exercised an influence as models, as they certainly existed as forerunners, of the mist sublime part of the Divine Comedy, Dante's conception of Paradise, then Spain may be entitled to claim for her Moslem thinkers no slight share in the worldwide fame enjoyed by the immortal work of Dante Alighieri.[33]

Furthermore, Palacios asserts on the similarities between the story of the *Mi'raj* and Dante's work:

> What is obvious is, that in none of the so-called precursors of the *Divine Comedy* could Dante find so typical a model as the Moslem legend Version A. Beatrice, human indeed, but rendered angelic through the Beatific Vision, descends from heaven with divine permission to conduct Dante to the Throne of God. Through space

they fly; and likewise Gabriel leads Mahomet. In both ascensions the travellers pass through the astronomical heavens, tarrying awhile in each to converse with the blessed and receive enlightenment on theological problems. The prophets in the Moslem heavens are the saints in Dante's poem. The literary artifice in both works is identical, no matter how they differ in art and spiritual detail.[34]

The analogies of the *mi'raj* story and Dante's work were also concurred in 1949 by the Spanish orientalist J. Munoz Sendino and Italian Enrico Cerulli. According to Saccone, they "pointed to the many-fold detailed or structural analogies between this Islamic holy legend and Dante's poem: cosmographical descriptions; the role of the Angel-Accompanier; particulars of the punishment of the damned, etc."[35] While Palacios accepted Dante's imitation of the legend, Sendino and Cerulli asserted the originality of the Florentine poet's work.

Renewed interest in the Pseudo-Dionysius theology of a mystic whose belief was that God is an "incomprehensible and inaccessible light" was a preoccupation during the medieval and Renaissance periods.[36] Dante's journey and his search for righteousness affect not only the spiritual, but also the scripture. St. Paul in Acts writes, "Whereupon as I journeyed to Damascus with the authority and commission of the chief priests, at midday, O king, I saw on the way a light from heaven, above the brightness of the sun, shining round about me and them that journeyed with me," the morality of the journey seeming to be confirmed by the appearance of light within scripture.[37] Dante the Pilgrim, in the *Divine Comedy* is on a journey, beginning in the darkness of Hell and ending in the light of Heaven.[38] According to Barolsky,

When Michelangelo wrote in his famous late sonnet "Giunto e gia 'l corso della vita mia" [Already my life has run its course], in which he describes the journey of his life over stormy seas in a frail bark to the common port through which all souls must pass, his language resonated with Dante's *navicella* [little boat] or *piccioletta barca* [little bark], with Dante's aspiration to reach the *glorioso porto* [glorious port] beyond the *gran mare dell'essere* [great sea of being], and when he sent the poem to Vasari in the autumn of 1554, he secured its eventual inclusion in his own Dantesque biography, which is the story of the journey of the artist as pilgrim from darkness and error to light and perfection.[39]

From this viewpoint it is plausible to state that Dante had either direct or indirect access to the story of the *mi'raj*. According to Marie-Rose Séguy from the Bibliotheque Nationale, "Apart from the existence of these translations, the many references to the *Mi'raj* in writings of the time allow us to think that Dante may at any rate have had some knowledge of Moslem eschatology."[40]

Michelangelo was familiar with the Biblical scripture and Dante's poetry. One of the artist's contemporary biographers, Giorgio Vasari's (1511-1574) claimed that he "delighted in scripture," and also confirmed the influence of Dante's poetry.[41] As a young man, Michelangelo often read Petrarch, Dante, or Boccaccio.[42] His reading of Dante is thought to have been his most intensive.[43] One of Michelangelo's Roman contemporary, Donato Gianotti (1492-1573), praised the artist as a great *dantista*.[44] Michelangelo, in one of his sonnets "Dante", writes of the loss of Dante to the afterlife and of his ascension to heaven:

What should be said of him cannot be said; / By too great splendor is his name attended ... / This man descended to the doomed and dead / For our instruction; then to God ascended; / Heaven opened wide to him its portals splendid...[45]

Here, Michelangelo explores the theme of losing someone who has served as the artist's earthly inspiration. The idea of the ascension of the body to the next world exemplified here by Michelangelo resonates in both Christian and Islamic belief systems. And, having read Dante's works, Michelangelo, indirectly may have been influenced by Islamic eschatology. Michelangelo explores the light of Christ in his Second Coming to judge the souls at the end of times in the *Last Judgement.*

For Sinan, too, through his piety makes a number of references to the night journey in his autobiographies. Sinan, as a janissary in the Ottoman army belonged to the Bektashi Sufi order. In his autobiographies he states, "I attained maturity in the hearth of Haci Bektaş [d. 1271]."[46] Sufi mysticism shaped his perceptions of himself and his art. Sufi philosophy expressed in Sinan's writings invite the observer on a journey of theophanic experience to witness his art as an expression of the visible manifestations of God to humanity and ponder on his salvation. Sinan alludes to the metaphysical nature of his art by comparing it to the Prophet's ascension (*mi'raj*) to different levels of heaven and finally meeting God at the "Utmost boundary" (53:14).[47] Witnessing the Imaginal World of Angels and other spirits by Muhammad, complement the Qur'anic message of hope of an afterlife. This message further inspired Muslim artists, including Sinan, to evoke this transcendental experience of the world to come for the observer in their art. This transcendental experience of the *mi'raj* provides hope and salvation for the individual seeking *ittihad* (Union with God) through the intercession of the Prophet. In his autobiographies Sinan states:

> And because that Beloved of God was the cause of all Creation, on the Night of the Prophet's miraculous ascent to the Throne of God, [that] seal of the seal ring, signet of intercession, and joyful crown was exalted and celebrated with the jewelled ornament [...][48]

References to ascension, jewels and ornaments of paradise, and Throne of God, stimulate the artist's imagination to create works of art to evoke this Imaginal World. Sinan then continues to allude to his works in Istanbul "to be lofty like the heavens" similar to the paradisiacal wonders experienced by Muhammad.[49] From this viewpoint, the works of the artist enhances the theophanic experience for the observer.

The theophanic experience becomes the convergent point between Michelangelo and Sinan – seeking God through their respective artwork and, finding hope and salvation in the world to come. It is the convergence of the stories of Prophet Muhammad's *Mi'raj* and Dante's *Divine Comedy* inspired the two Renaissance masters of the Age. Michelangelo's and Sinan's works require contemplation and reflection allowing the observer to grow intellectually, and to make sense of his / her world. The eighth century Arab historian Ibn Ishaq (704-768) sums up the metaphorical message of the ascension in the following words that also reinforces the underlying connotations articulated in Michelangelo's *Last Judgment* and Sinan's *çini* aesthetics in the Rustem Pasha Mosque:

The matter of the place of the journey and what is said about it is the searching test and a matter of God's power and authority wherein is a lesson for the intelligent; and guidance and mercy and strengthening to those who believe.[50]

All artworks are reflections of human spiritual depth. Whether the art is the fresco of Michelangelo or the *çini* of Sinan, they represent a reflection of thoughts and feelings existent in the human spirit. Artistic sophistication of the Renaissance and elegance always goes in parallel with spiritual perceptiveness. Thematically, it is here, that the art of the aesthetics of Michelangelo meets the art of the aesthetics of Sinan.

CHAPTER 5

MICHELANGELO MEETS SINAN

ANAGOGICAL AND ESCHATOLOGICAL READINGS OF THE 'LAST JUDGEMENT' AND THE IZNIK ÇİNİ OF THE RUSTEM PASHA MOSQUE

A comparison of two apparently dissimilar works of art, the *Last Judgement* and the Rustem Pasha Mosque, may appear fruitless. However, it quickly becomes apparent that, thematically, the works share similar subject matter; both seeking to capture the Last Day and the afterlife, either in the Paradise or Hell of Christian and Islamic eschatology. On a literal level, Michelangelo's fresco reflects on 'judgement', and thus, both condemnation and salvation by Christ, while Sinan's mosque posits that Paradise and salvation are available to those who possess faith and open their hearts and minds to God's Signs. However, on a figurative level, an anagogical interpretation reveals much deeper insights into the works as through their creation, both artists moved towards a more abstract style of representing the Divine, salvation and Paradise. Stylistically, for Michelangelo, it is the enlarged, twisted and dwarfed figures (*contrapposto*) on the altar wall, which represent a way of reacting to the harmonious ideals associated with other Renaissance artists, such as Leonardo da Vinci and Raphael. For Sinan, on the other hand, as an observer moves about the mosque interior—both from a distance and at close range—the abstract floral arrays displayed on the Iznik tiles oscillate from being images that are both clear and unclear. That is, while the tiles'

design may initially appear obvious, the closer one gets to the tiles the more abstract they become. The results of the two artists' High Renaissance Mannerist styles unite them as master artists, and the ambiguities of their works require closer inspection, that is, from their respective cultural and historical contexts.[1]

Both Christianity and Islam professed to the idea of life after death. Medieval Muslim scholars debated the issue of the immortality of the soul since they came into contact with the works of Aristotle. In the twelfth century Ibn Rushd (Averroes) questioned the authority of Aristotle the mortality of individual souls. Instead, he posited a kind of collective immortality, "persons [are] immortal insofar as they participate in the transcendental intellect, an entity that is spiritual and immaterial, as well as immortal."[2] Renaissance humanists like Marsilio Ficino could not accept this medieval Islamic view of the soul. In 1482 Ficino, as Hall states, "grounded personal immortality in the humanist tenets of the dignity of humankind, our central position in the cosmos, and our desire to be like God."[3] The controversy over the nature of human soul continued when other leading theologians like Tommaso de Vio, known as Cajetan was philosophically closer to Averroes's interpretation when he presented his argument to Pope Julius II in 1503 pronouncing that, "although the doctrine could not be proven by reason, it must be accepted as an article of faith based on scripture".[4] As St. Paul in his letter 1 Corinthians 15:49 writes: "Just as we have borne the image of the man of dust [that is, Adam] we shall also bear the image of the man of heaven". Citing Paul from the scripture Cajetan writes: "Our body in the resurrection is compared without hyperbole to a celestial body."[5]

While St. Paul did not address himself with the question of the resurrection of the sinners and their appearance in the afterlife, Cajetan did. He argues that "The bodies of the Damned will be imperishable with no use [need] of sex or food or body fluids, but they will not be glorified and insensitive to pain."[6] According to Hall this remark by the theologian must have been of "great help to Michelangelo" and his representation of the sinners in the Last Judgement.[7] Looking back to the ancient Greek ideas which dominated humanism, and which saw the youthful virile male as the ideal, Michelangelo's idealized youthful nude seemed the most appropriate forms this celestial body takes in the afterlife. By idealising the Elect, the Damned were represented as being tormented and anguished but most importantly without the loss of their humanity.

These theological debates during the Renaissance explain the non-traditional actions of the figures depicted by Michelangelo. As the Renaissance humanists, such as Ficino, failed to reconcile scripture with the Platonic canon of the 'immortality of the soul', the Neo-Platonic order—where the body is placed below the soul—"clashed irreconcilably with the biblical view of man as a psychosomatic unity."[8] Accordingly, Hall views the debate of Renaissance humanists as a denigration of the body and as being at odds with Paul's biblical affirmation of it. However, Michelangelo's *Last Judgement* clearly affirms the latter, in which the human figures "are the most emphatically corporeal figures he had ever created."[9]

Similarly, the Ottomans, too, engaged in the Renaissance debate regarding the nature of salvation and the world to come in the Platonic sense. With the Prophet's intercession, noted above, Sinan assures that salvation is attainable. Sinan then continues to allude to his works in Istanbul "to be lofty like the heavens."[10] This way the works of the artist enhances the theophanic experience for the observer. For Sinan, Ottoman Renaissance art came to represent the Ottoman paradise on earth as a signpost of the next life. He compares his art to "nightingales" inviting all to the "rose garden", the "celestial throne", "Milky Way", as experienced by the Prophet on his Night Journey.[11] Entering a mosque built by Sinan is like entering a "rose garden" whose doors "are like those of Paradise" where the seeker can wash his sins away from the "pool of Kevser, that matchless fountain to be."[12] Like the whirling dervish and the pilgrim circumambulating the Ka'ba during the *hajj* pilgrimage seeking union with God, Sinan, too, affirms that the observer will find salvation, mercy and be absolved of his sins by "Circling the rose garden of the sanctuary … Comes there [his mosques] to win God's blessing" and "free from hellfire secure."[13] With this classical mindset, Sinan's Renaissance outlook in the Rustem Pasha

Mosque explores the world to come through the art of Iznik aesthetics. Like Michelangelo, he provides the visitor glimpses of salvation in the hereafter and the Qur'anic paradise through a theophanic and esoteric experience.

Aesthetics of Michelangelo and Sinan: Representations of Salvation

According to Shearman the *Last Judgement* fresco was in fact "an autonomous spiritual and artistic entity."[14] For Anne Leader, "Michelangelo's fresco completes the chapel's proclamation of the pope's unique role as temporal and spiritual ruler who provides the needed conduit to God and salvation."[15] Similarly, the ostentatious nature of the Rustem Pasha Mosque interior attests to Sultan Süleyman's messianic mission to establish an Ottoman *paradise* on earth.[16] The abstract naturalism expressed in the tiles, which were inspired by the vivid imageries of Paradise as presented in Qur'anic verses, affirms the sultanate's construct of an earthly paradise where the mosque became just one of many symbols through the conduit of the sultan.

The *Last Judgement* complements the decoration of the entire chapel by completing the biblical narrative of the ceiling and the walls of the Sistine Chapel. However, an anagogical reading of the altar fresco not only offers insight into the eschatological debate that was taking place during the Renaissance, but also provides art historians with an awareness of Michelangelo's psychological struggle; of his fear about his salvation. Thus, the tension and ambiguity created by the artist has long dominated the debate regarding the true nature of the *Last Judgement*. However, the apocalyptic tone of the fresco may represent the end of the era of Humanism and the beginning of the Counter-Reformation.[17] For Marcia Hall, it is this condemnatory tone that has traditionally been interpreted as, "a rejection of the confidence in man so powerfully conveyed by Michelangelo himself twenty-two years earlier in the Sistine vault overhead."[18] Hall believes that it has been more convenient for art historians to view the fresco through the definition of Mannerism, rather than the one narrative of the Sistine vault connecting with the altar wall narrative of the High Renaissance, because by the middle of the sixteenth century Michelangelo had moved into more abstract forms of representations. While other medieval 'Last Judgements' in the Strozzi Chapel (1354- 9) depict figures dressed according to their social hierarchy, Michelangelo created a new standard *(Figure 11)*.

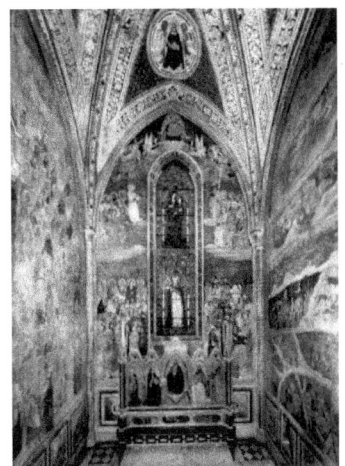

Figure 11. 'The Last Judgement' in the Strozzi Chapel, (1354-1359) by Andrea di Cione, Basilica of Santa Maria Novella. Photograph by Metin Mustafa, October, 1999.

Through his use of nudity, he created equality among all the figures that were depicted as awaiting judgement. Such *metaphysical anxiety* created in these sacred spaces allow for contemplation of one's mortality. According to Paul Klee (1879-1940), the Swiss-German painter:

> At the root of this inner distress [i.e., metaphysical anxiety] lies the defeat (or rather the retreat) of consciousness. In the upsurge of mystical experience, everything that once bound man to the human world, to earth, to time and space, to matter and the natural living of life, has been cast aside or dissolved.[19]

With the dissolving of all earthly forms, desires and connections to the world, opens the path to transcendental doorway. Michelangelo achieves this theophanic experience through the portrayal of the separation of the blessed—who would enter Heaven—from the damned by showing the saved souls ascending on the left of Christ's celestial kingdom and the damned descending on the right, to Hell.

Michelangelo's *Last Judgement* represents the idea of life after death according to the Christian tradition. At a literal level, the work depicts the Second Coming of Christ and the Final Judgement of all humanity as declared in the Book of Revelations in the New Testament. The souls of people rise and descend to their fates, as judged by Christ, surrounded by prominent saints who have died cruel deaths, including Catherine of Alexandria, Peter, Lawrence, Bartholomew, Paul, Sebastian and John the Baptist. From past interpretations of the fresco to the ambiguity of contemporary analyses of Christ's actions, for example, whether he is just or vengeful, have led to much debate. According to Steinberg, rather than admitting to ambiguity, which may signify disrespect towards Michelangelo's ability to express himself clearly, most scholars have concluded that, "Michelangelo cast the Christ of the Second Coming in a posture which cannot be matched in our vocabulary or analogized to normal physical habits."[20] From such a perspective the figure of Christ represents "otherworldliness"[21] and the uncertainty that awaits us. Therefore, because the fresco depicts a moment immediately "before"[22] Judgement, i.e. before any knowledge of what awaits the believer after death, the dramatic tension of the piece is amplified. The notion of being reborn anew is depicted by the unfamiliar Renaissance imagery of a beardless Christ, as the New Adam, where Michelangelo makes a connection to the first man created by God on the ceiling of the Chapel. For Hall, it is precisely this notion of being reborn—or the resurrection of the body—that the *Last Judgement* embodies. For Hall, the Renaissance context of the many Last Judgement paintings suggested that, "[r]esurrection was not that of Christ, which was already represented in its logical place in the life of the Christ frescoes on the walls, rather it was to represent the Christian doctrine of the Resurrection of the Body."[23] Seeing the fresco of Michelangelo from these eschatological perspectives provide insight into the mind of the artist, as well as the political and religious climate of the Counter-Reformation period. This is reinforced in St. Paul 1, Corinthians 15, from the New Testament— "Now if this is what we proclaim, that Christ was raised from the dead, how can some of you say there is no resurrection of the dead?"[24]

Like Michelangelo's *Last Judgement*, the Mosque of Rustem Pasha would serve as a reminder to worshippers of their spiritual needs and their existence in the larger, cosmological scheme of things. During the sixteenth century, Sinan's move toward floral naturalism was the first step in what became an Ottoman-Turkish artistic genre. As the trend toward naturalism became more refined and sophisticated in early modern Ottoman art, stylised flowers became dominant motifs. Sinan's use of blossoms, brilliant red tulips, and carnations make their appearance at the Mosque of Rustem Pasha and are placed on the walls of the mosque in recurring patterns. Together, the floral motifs signify the Islamic concept of *zikr*—the remembrance of God through prayer and contemplation, which often incorporates the use of prayer beads (*Figures 11a-c*).[25] In fact, the sheer number of flowers in the floral depictions symbolise the Qur'anic verse in 17:110, "His are the most beautiful names," as well as the beauty and wonder of His creation on earth, reinforcing the contemporary historian Ramazanzade's words for the description of the mosque—a "noble sanctuary" resembling the "fourth heaven" as witnessed by Prophet Muhammad during his *Mir'aj* experience.[26]

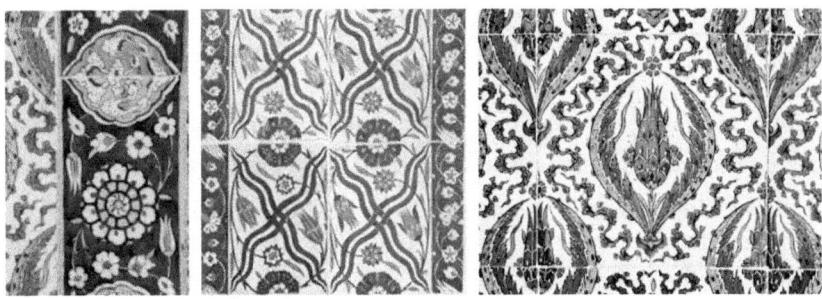

Figures 11a-c. Iznik tile details of the Rustem Pasha Mosque depicting the variations of tulips, roses and other flowers. Together, the floral motifs signify the Islamic concept of zikr—the remembrance of God through prayer and contemplation, which often incorporates the use of prayer beads. In fact, the sheer number of flowers in the floral depictions symbolise the Qur'anic verse in 17:110, 'His are the most beautiful names', as well as the beauty and wonder of His creation on earth.' Photographs by Metin Mustafa, January 20, 2015.

The floral motifs demonstrate a specific visual language that is tied to Iznik çini design and the Qur'an. Two explanations shed light on these symbolic representations. The first is attributed to the visual representation of Qur'anic calligraphy. The Iznik cursive patterns of serrated edged leaves, the *saz* style, after its originator Şahkulu (d. 1556), with other fantastic foliage bearing large composite blossoms and long feathery leaves allude to the arabesque lettering of the Qur'an. The combination of the Qur'anic inscriptions and the Iznik *çini* decorative aesthetics adorning the interior design of Ottoman mosques act as reminders of God's Word and the visual depiction of the promised paradise to believers beneath which rivers flow (Qur'an, 18:31). Like their Renaissance counterparts in the Latin West, the Ottoman artists, similarly created on a grand-scale paradisiacal canvasses that requires anagogical interpretation.

Secondly, the floral patterns further augment the religious symbolisms that are associated with the Iznik *çini*. The tulip motif is primarily depicted as sitting flaccid, symbolising the submission of the believer to Allah, whilst the rose is shown in full bloom to indicate praise for His creation in a display of the Almighty's glory. During the sixteenth century the Turkish word *lâle* (tulip) became an anagram of the Muslim term for Allah, as the letters in *lâle* are also contained in the word for Al-lah, meaning The One.[27] More than forty variations of tulip motifs can be found within the mosque. Like the prayer beads in which every bead is a reminder of God's attributes during prayer time, so too in this sacred space every tulip represents God and acts as a reminder of Him. Like the dominating figure of Christ in the *Last Judgement* fresco in the Sistine Chapel, the dispersal of tulips throughout the mosque also symbolises the omnipresence of God, and reminds the individual that, "He is with you wherever you are" (*Figures 11d-e*).[28]

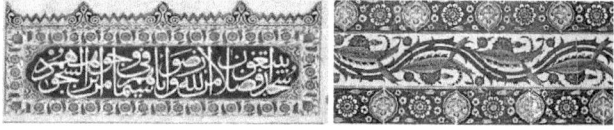

Figures 11d, 11e. Above, Qur'anic wall inscription on Iznik tiles in mosques; below Iznik tiles with floral and foliage designs in the Rustem Pasha Mosque stressing the connection between the Qur'anic cursive script and the visual representation of the Word of God by the Iznik çini. Photographs by Metin Mustafa, October 2019.

Like the tulip, the rose or *gül* had mystical overtones. The ancient Europeans believed the rose to have come from the blood of the goddess Venus. Similarly, Ogier Ghiselinde Busbecq (1555), the Austrian ambassador to the court of Süleyman the Magnificent, discussed the Ottomans' belief that the rose had been born form the sweat of the Prophet.[29] This mystical association is also referenced by the thirteenth-century dervish poet Yunus Emre's (1240–1320): "the flower is he, that dervish rose is Muhammad's sweat."[30] Thus, in Sufi symbolism the rose came to represent Divine beauty and the face of the "beloved," His Prophet. It also entered Islamic mystical literature as the "flower of blood" and the "flower of suffering" to highlight the torment that the Prophet endured to deliver the Divine message to his people. It also came to symbolise the soul in search of the Divine just as Rustem Pasha's soul would do in his journey to the Hereafter.[31] The personified rose in Sufi poetry calls out to God, as the poet Yunus Emre writes, "and in the garden scent of roses is wafting, declaring God's name."[32] When combined in floral arrangements, the two types of flowers—tulips and roses—evoke the first pillar of Islam: "there is no God but God, and Muhammad is the Messenger of God." As J. M. Rogers and R. M. Ward claim, Iznik floral imagery imbued with religious significance accentuated the Sufi mystical reading associated with the tile aesthetics.[33]

Within the courtyard of the mosque, religious inscriptions of white cursive *thuluth* script on Iznik tiles, by the gifted court calligrapher, Ahmet Karahısarı, adorn the window tops along the enclosures. Qur'anic inscriptions are also used, and set the tone of the mosque, they read: "He is Allah, the Creator, the Shaper out of naught, the Fashioner. His are the most beautiful names. All that is in the heavens and the earth glorifieth Him, and He is the Mighty, the Wise."[34] The placement of the panels on either side of the main door symbolise the entrance to Paradise on the Day of Judgement, where the believers, just as the angels, "will enter upon them from every gate [with the salutation]: 'Peace be upon you for you have been patient. Excellent indeed is your final abode.'"[35] Similarly, in the *Last Judgement*, the otherworldly nature of the larger than life Christ figure—suspended in mid-air in the centre of the fresco—with his demanding and overpowering presence over the elect, his mother, angels and the damned, signifies a doorway to the next world. Thus, this Paradise is open for all who seek His mercy and forgiveness to enter. Unfortunately, only the left panel remains intact in the present day with "blossoming spring trees of manganese-purple springing from cluster of large leaves with sawtooth-like edges. The leaves are shown in a wind-blown movement and decorated with thin hyacinth sprays."[36]

On the remaining surface of the panel there is a plethora of different flowers. The large leaves at the bottom of the panel envelope a pair of tulips and the same flower is repeated elsewhere on the panel, but with different petals. Flanking the trees at the bottom are sprays of tiny spring flowers, and between the trees are a rosebud and a rose with a swirling red centre, with white hyacinths gathered on the left side. Among other stylised flowers arranged on the entrance panel of the Mosque of Rustem Pasha, at various orientations, are carnations. Along with the tulip, the carnation was another flower that was poetically employed to recall Divine Beauty and evoke spiritual contemplation. For the medieval Andalusian Sufi philosopher Ibn Arabi (1165-1240) "[…] this theophanic function of Beauty will present the most perfect image of Divinity" and provide comfort and hope for the seeker.[37] It is, thus, the art of Iznik that acts as a reminder of the world to come and allow the individual to 'remould' his soul in order to recognise *tawhid* and perhaps attain *ittihad* through this theophanic experience. To the right are several lotus or peony buds and two rosette-shaped floras. Chinese cloud bands can be seen at the top and bottom of the panel, and resemble the energetic form of the dragon, which in Ottoman symbolism represents the fire from the beak of the mythical bird, the *simurg*—similar to the phoenix in Western tradition —depicted widely in miniature paintings.[38] The *simurg* can also be seen in court literature in which it is described as resurrecting itself after death, to begin life anew, and denotes "maturity in mystical sense and intimacy with God."[39] Thus, by entering this sacred site, one is demonstrating wisdom and seeking the spiritual relationship with the Divine for which the soul yearns. In addition to the motifs already discussed, there is an undulating red band at the top of the panel with rectangular knots derived from metal work. Large *rumis* decorate the spandrels outside the lobed arch and include split-leaves and *palmettes*, which symbolise both life and death.[40] Throughout these adornments runs a thin vine-scroll with tiny leaves that wind through the panel, and on this panel one can see a rare example of turquoise, which has been ground in the revetments, thereby, reinforcing its significance in the artistry of sixteenth century Iznik tile decoration. Their similarity to Michelangelo's use of spandrels in the Sistine Chapel has led scholars, such as Denny, to suggest that this panel and the interior wall decorations represent "for the first time an elaborate program of decoration in which there was a massive attempt in many places to coordinate the actual manufacture of the tile revetments very meticulously with the wall surfaces of the building itself" *(Figures 12, 13).*[41]

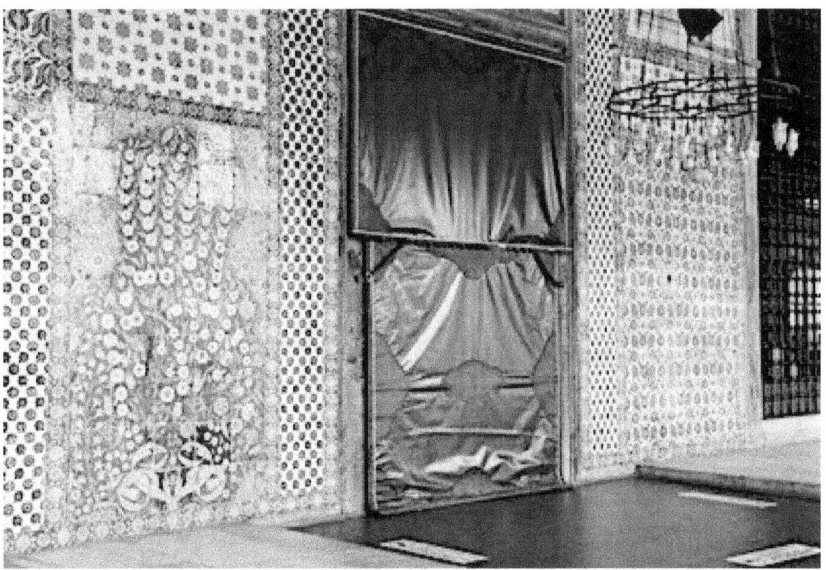

Figure 12. Right, The tile panels on either side of the entrance of the Rustem Pasha Mosque c.1560-61.

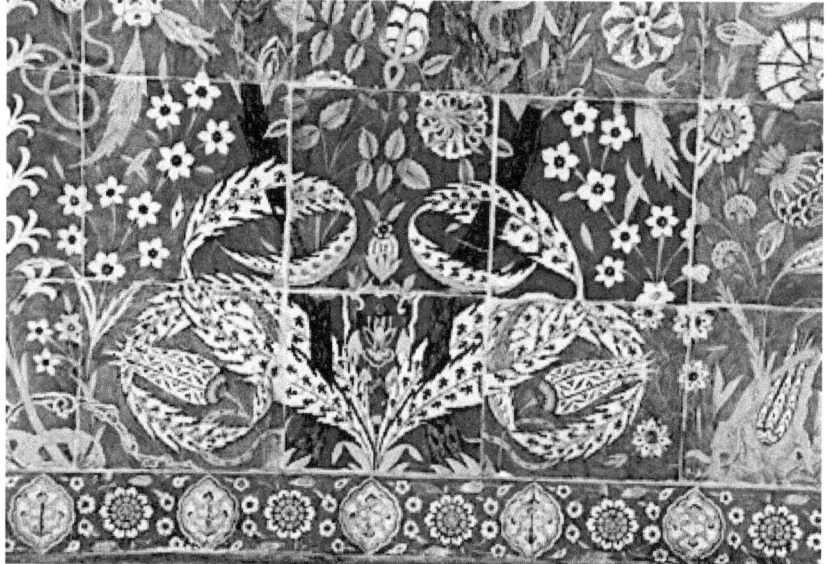

Figure 13. Below, detail of the left entrance panel. The manganese-purple can be seen in the bottom right panel surrounding the tulip. Due to its poor visibility from a distance the use of this colour was abandoned by the Iznik artists. Photographs by Metin Mustafa, December 13, 2014.

The vivid details of the Iznik tiles at the entrance of the mosque bring to mind the following Qur'anic verses:

They shall dwell in the gardens of Eden, with rivers rolling at their feet [...] They will be among thorn-less lote-trees [...] in long-extended shade, by constantly flowing water [...][42]

The blossoming tree with *palmettes* is intertwined with the intricate vine-scroll that runs through the tile panel narrative, and expresses one's good and evil attributes. As with the allegory of the *simurg*, it also conveys and intimacy with the Creator, and provides the observer with a sense of hope of finding Paradise. Additionally, this juxtaposition of human attributes is a direct link with Sufi beliefs, as Rumi wrote, "[s]ometimes angels envy our cleanliness and sometimes the devils run away from our evil [...] What a mysterious creature is man that different habits, virtues, goodness and evil come together in him."[43] Likewise, within the Rustem Pasha Mosque, human subjects stand to make a spiritual decision, that is, whether to enter the mosque and seek salvation. Within Sufism and according to Rumi, in order to do this one must be able to look within and acknowledge mistakes, that is, look through the 'ego of the *nafs*' (i.e. the ego of the self). Once this has been accomplished, Sufism asserts that His Light will bless the individual and angels will worship him God as His viceroy on earth chooses Man.[44] In applying this to the design of the Rustem Pasha Mosque, it appears that such salvation begins at its entry, where the floral arrangements and blossoming tree provide hope and a sense of temporary relief from worldly desires, at which point one is able to examine his actions and look through the ego of the self. Sinan's work expresses an aesthetic that echo in Rumi's (d.1273) famous words:

Come, come, whoever you are: Wanderer, worshiper, lover of leaving. It doesn't matter. Ours is not a caravan of despair. Come, even if you have broken your vows a thousand times. Come, yet again, come, come.[45]

Even if one has 'broken his vows a thousand times' as stated by Rumi above, one cannot lose hope of salvation and God's forgiveness. This existentialist angst is also felt in the self-fashioning of Sultan Süleyman (d. 1566) that is reflected in the mosque aesthetics. Poetry composed by Süleyman at the time of the construction of the mosque reflects his own spiritual and self-reflective tone:

If you aspire to God's compassion, kindness should come from you too; be sure to offer your benevolence and mercy to people of virtue. If you hope to reach the gardens of Paradise to find love and grace. Instead of terrifying destruction when the end comes to

you, humble yourself like a skirt[46], bow at the sage's feet and rub
your face.[47]

Just as Sinan's Iznik aesthetics offer the visitor the moment to reflect,
Süleyman, too, in his poem reinforces a similar message. To "reach the
gardens of Paradise", the visitor can find salvation, love, grace, kindness and mercy in this sacred space.

Like Rumi asking all those who broke their promises to God thousands
of times to come to His presence again and again, Süleyman, too,
advises the visitor on a journey of transformation to humble himself
before the One. In other words, hope and salvation come with the
sincerity and true intentions of the believer who submits to the One,
even after a thousand sins.

*Aesthetics of Michelangelo and Sinan: art as metaphors for self-
reflection*

Unlike the Sufi view of sinners, the *Last Judgement's* representations of
the damned (to the left of Christ) allow for consideration before salvation is attained. Michelangelo's decision to cover the entire wall of the
altar without the use of a frame suggests an infinite space, in another
time and dimension, which transforms the viewer into a participant
within the Last Judgement; requiring self-examination and reflection
one's life and place on the apocalyptic day. The fresco also alludes to
Dante and the poems of Michelangelo himself. As Sarah Melanie Rolfe
suggests, "[i]t would appear that Michelangelo, who was acquainted
with both the *Commedia* and Landino's interpretations of the epic,
chose to include the famous literary scholar's allegorical interpretations of *Inferno III* and *V* into his *Last Judgment.*"[48] In Dante's *Inferno*,
Minos "descended from the first circle into the second, that less space
begirds, and so much greater dole that goads to wailing. There
standeth Minos, horribly, and snarls: Examines the transgressions at
the entrance; Judges, and sends according as he girds him."[49] In Landino's (1425-1498) analysis of Dante's Minos, he is presented as the
conscience of the damned man because, according to Landino, there is
nothing more threatening than the sins of an individual and their

guilty conscience. According to Rolfe, this allegorical interpretation of Minos is consistent with Steinberg's interpretation of Hell in Michelangelo's *Last Judgement*: "It is not smart of the sensible body nor fear of the pangs to come that torment, but horror of abysmal guilt [...] the pains of Hell are but the shame and remorse of the sinner made aware of his state."[50] This sentiment resonates with the metaphorical "undying worm" that is mentioned in the Gospel of Mark 9:44, where torture and torment is not physical, but rather, psychological. Interestingly, however, there is no depiction of Hell in the fresco. Loren Partridge suggests that it is the fresco that is ambiguous, and that ambiguity "reflects the Italian movement for Church reform."[51] Furthermore, Partridge believes that in order to understand this ambiguity one must look at both the literary influences of the time and one's own personal struggle.

The influence of Dante's work in Michelangelo's *Last Judgement* can also be seen with the character of Charon, who appears in the fresco as well as the poet's *Inferno*—carrying the damned across the Acheron to Hell.[52] According to Landino, Charon denotes choice and volition: "the Acheron is the means by which the soul passes into sin, Charon is free will, the ship is volition, and the oar is choice."[53] Considering Landino's figurative interpretations of Minos and Charon, the individual arriving in Hell in Michelangelo's *Last Judgement* suggests, according to Rolfe, "the misuse of free will to a guilty and punishing conscience [which] after death ultimately becomes punishment in Hell."[54] Michelangelo's reference to Genesis and the serpent, who tempts the first man, is obvious. His inner struggle appears to have driven him to curse the world for his birth, and his free will—which led him to 'pick the forbidden fruit' and succumb to temptation. However, Michelangelo also appears to have believed that only the Light of God could save him: "O Lord, break down that wall / which with its hardness keeps delayed from us / the sun of your light, extinguished in this world. / Send that promised light, which we will see someday, / to your beautiful bride, so that my heart / may burn free from any doubt, and feel only you."[55] Beseeching God to shed His Light upon him so that he may find peace and resolve his inner demons is a sentiment that resonates in the hope of salvation, which Michelangelo also expressed in his depiction of the Second Coming of Christ, in the *Last Judgement*.

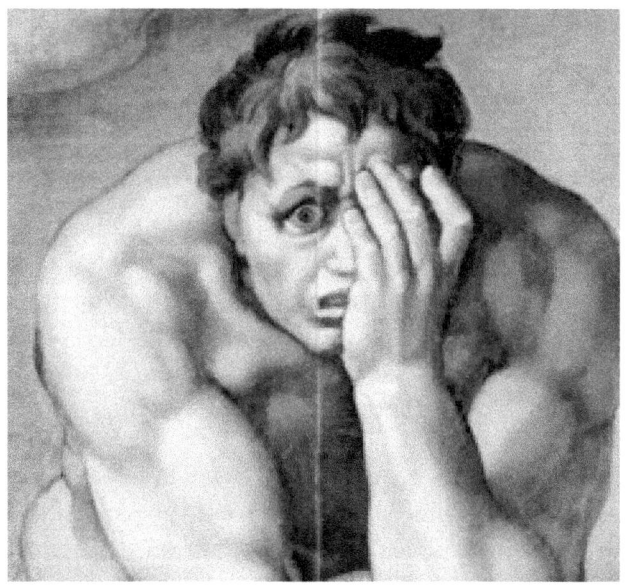

Figure 14. Photograph of the detail from Michelangelo's 'Last Judgement'. Photograph reproduction.

The conscience of the fresco's damned figure, with his face in his hands while lamenting his fate, alludes to Michelangelo's agony as a man who, like most, was unprepared to meet his Lord and face Divine judgement *(Figure 14)*.

Like Rumi and according to Sufi philosophy, Michelangelo's poetry also alludes to this mirror of the self, as expressed in the following lines:

Alas, alas, I have been betrayed / by my fleeting days and by the mirror / that speaks the truth to all who look hard at it! / That's what happens when one delays too long at the end, / as I have done, while time has fled from me: / he finds himself in one day, as I have, old. / And I can neither repent, nor pre- pare myself, / nor ask for guidance, with death so near to me.[56]

Therefore, the *Last Judgement* can be read as a representation of an 'inner mirror' of the self, coming face-to-face with one's sins and facing one's Jungian "shadow" to discover the authentic self.[57]

Like his Renaissance counterpart, Sinan also uses the concept of an 'inner mirror' as a metaphor for self-reflection, which is clear in his interior aesthetics of the Rustem Pasha Mosque. This self-reflection for spiritual and intellectual growth echoes Ibn Ishaq's words above. While there are no angelic figures in Sinan's visual medium, his use of invocation on Iznik tiles and the anti-*qibla* wall express, as noted by Hall (above), a similar angst to that felt when viewing the *Last Judgement*. The words on the window lunettes of Sinan's mosque read: "O God! Remove us from the Fire and make us enter Paradise together with the righteous ones by showing your mercy. O, the most merciful of all!"[58] Similarly, another invocation pleads for Divine help in both this world and the next: "O God! Give us forgiveness and health in the world and the Hereafter".[59] These supplications on the lunettes express similar messages as Michelangelo's figures who are both ascending to Heaven and descending into Hell.

Additionally, Sinan represents 'self-examination' and 'reflection' through the use of the *mihrab* – the sacred focal point of the *qibla* wall. There is a symbolic relationship between the *mihrab* aesthetics and the *Äyat al-nur* (the Light Verse, Quran 24: 35) where the Light of God guides all those who seek it:

Allah is the Light of the heavens and the earth. The example of His light is like a niche with in which is a lamp, The lamp is within glass, the glass as if it were a pearly [white] star, Lit from [the oil of] a blessed olive tree, Neither of the east nor of the west, Whose oil would almost glow even if untouched by fire. Light upon light.

> Allah guides to His Light whom He wills. And Allah presents examples for the people, and Allah is Knowing of all things.[60]

It can be argued that there is the supposition that *mihrab* is the representation of God's Light as it symbolises the hope of salvation prompting self-reflection.[61] Furthermore, Sinan's religious references to his work alludes to closeness to God and Paradise, "exalted mihrab is the confidant of the names of God. Its every corner is a rose garden of Paradise with adornments of the springtime."[62] Engulfed on all sides by the rose garden of Paradise and in close proximity to God stimulate the sensory perceptions of the individual seeking spiritual enlightenment for "Allah guides to His Light whom He wills."

The striking features of the *mihrab* revetment inside the Rustem Pasha Mosque consist of five identical panels and perfectly fit the space reserved for them (*Figures 15a-b*). The artistic feature of each panel includes a blossoming spring tree that is enclosed in a large blue ground cartouche, budding from a vase that faces the worshipper, thus, creating the appearance of the Garden of Paradise. The intensity of the colours of the *mihrab* tiles plays a crucial role in the mosque interior decorative aesthetics that stimulate the senses and provide an ethereal experience as one is drawn to the centre of this sacred space. Like Goethe's theory of the emotional effect of colour on the individual noted above, the Russian abstract painter and art theorist, Wassily Kandinsky (1866-1944), in his 1910 book, *Concerning the Spiritual in Art*, considers the powerful psychic effect of colour in the cohesive spiritual experience of art:

> The deeper the blue becomes, the more strongly it calls man towards the infinite, awakening in him a desire for the pure and, finally, for the supernatural. It is the color of the heavens, the same color we picture to ourselves when we hear the sound of the word "heaven" … The brighter it becomes, the more it loses its sound, until it turns into silent stillness and becomes white.[63]

This feeling of being drawn to the infinite, the pure and a place of peace is further accentuated by the tactile senses. Unlike the Sistine Chapel where the observer is prevented by the altar from getting close to the *Last Judgement* fresco allowing only the visual senses to stimulate the imagination, inside the Rustem Pasha mosque, the up close and personal with the Iznik *çini* further augments the theophanic experience for the individual. Moving one's fingers over the tulips, hyacinths, carnations, the serrated leaves and other flowers connect us directly with the floral symbols that represent the world of the Hereafter and the Infinite. As we symbolically connect between this world and the next, there arises from the visual and tactile experiences a more profound effect that occasions a deep emotional response. The sheer brilliance of the colours of the tiles activates a response that can be either spiritual or painful. As the geometric lines, curves of the leaves and different colours of blue, red and white of the *mihrab* merge into one another creating a hypnotic visual force, we begin to lose ourselves in their power as if drawing us closer to the Infinite. According to Kandinsky:

The psychological power of color ... call[s] forth a vibration from the soul. Its primary elementary physical power becomes simply the path which color reaches the soul ... Since in general the soul is closely connected to the body, it is possible that one emotional response may conjure up another, corresponding form of emotion by means of association ... [like] a spiritual vibration ... [or] exert a painful effect on the soul.[64]

The overwhelming psychological effect of the colours on the soul is subjective in nature and invites the individual for contemplation and self-reflection. Therefore, since the visual and tactile senses are stimulated by the art, it is the through the art that emotions are exerted prompting one to gain spiritual and inner awareness.

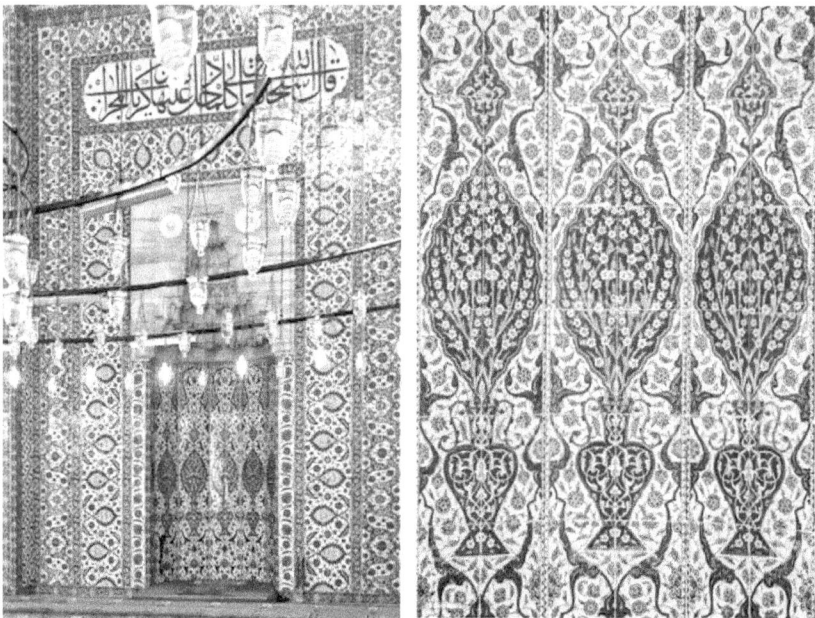

Figures 15a-b. Left, mihrab of the Rustem Pasha Mosque showing five identical panels; right, detail of the blossoming spring trees budding from vases inside the niche. Photographs by Metin Mustafa, December 13, 2014.

The intensity of the blue inside the *mihrab* is contrasted with the floral ensemble. The vase is filled with *rumi* designs, in white reserve on dark cobalt blue, and as noted by Cimok, "[t]he design is repeated in the spandrels of the lobed niche at the top. Large *rumi* leaves and a cartouche with cloud bands in white reserve on blue and *hatayi* blossoms with small leaves decorate the surface. The dark red, also used in the main border surrounding the *mihrab*, is rarely used in the mosque and is replaced by tomato red."[65] The five identical panels within the *mihrab* may signify the five daily prayers of the faithful. However, the use of the repetitive design on white reserve and the tomato red in the *mihrab* create a mesmerising waterfall- and shade-like effect, representing the two indispensable elements of Islamic gardens: water and shade. This allusion to the Garden of Eden becomes the focal point, with the dominant cobalt blue on all sides of the mosque's interior symbolising water—the life-giving force with the four rivers of Paradise flowing from its centre, the *mihrab*. This theme is mentioned in the Qur'an and in the *hadiths* of the Prophet's Night Journey in which the rivers run with water, milk, honey or wine.[66] Therefore, the symbol of water brings to life God's Beauty, as shown by the diversity of blossoming flowers in the vases. In fact, they not only allude to His Beauty, but also His Eden and His Creation.

The frame around the *mihrab* niche consists of tiles that use repeated designs. Some of these design patterns, such as the 'stippled' *saz* leaves that overlap and appear to move; dragon-like, as if blown by a strong wind, were never repeated in later Iznik tilework. The inner border is also composed of large *palmettes* with a pair of serrated leaves and draws one's eyes to the *mihrab*. Thus, for the worshipper, the *mihrab* and *qibla* signify that they are standing before the Almighty—in one-on-one dialogue with Him. Like Prophet Muhammad's *mir'aj*, this act symbolically represents the individual's own personal *mir'aj* achieving spiritual enlightenment and the hope of salvation. Aesthetically speaking Sinan achieves this effect by filling the *palmettes* with *rumis* giving "the impression of a richer texture" that is exemplified by the lusciousness of the Garden of Eden, "dark green in colour" expressed in the Qur'an.[67]

The *mihrab* acts like an *örtü* (a Turkish word meaning 'shawl' or 'veil'), and is an example of what Lisa Golombek has called the "draped universe".[68] Just as Süleyman achieved his "draped universe" by covering the exterior of the Dome of the Rock with tile revetments, which symbolically beautify and prepare the 'throne of God' for the Last Judgement of humanity,[69] in Sinan's internal draped world of the mosque an individual must first prepare oneself before s/he is called to answer for past deeds on the Last Day. The niche symbolises the spiritual compass of both the earthly direction of God's Light and where one should turn to reflection on one's daily actions. Likewise, Sinan's work does not contain the intense anguish that is displayed in Michelangelo's *Last Judgement*. Sinan leaves the sins of humanity for God, and God alone, to pardon, while allowing the individual standing before the *mihrab* to reflect upon their last judgement as death may come at any time. The *mihrab*, therefore, acts as reminder of the above Qur'anic verses, that is, how one will receive his / her Book of

Deeds on the Last Day. It allows for spiritual reflection on one's intimate connection to God and the degree of his earthly righteousness.
Like the figure of Muhammad and Gabriel standing before the tomato
red coloured arched gate of Paradise in Figure 9b, for the worshipper,
the *mihrab* becomes his / her own point of entry to the hereafter,
providing hope and salvation. As one stands before the *mihrab*,
through free will and His decree, it serves as a symbolic representation
of both one's freedom to choose within the pre-destiny of one's life.

Through the *mihrab* aesthetics, Sinan created a sense of apprehension,
within the observers of their own shortcomings on earth and to allow
for self-examination. Similarly, the Qur'an states:

Verily never will Allah (S) change the condition of a people until
they change what is in their hearts […] We will set up the scales of
justice for the day of resurrection, and no soul shall be treated
unjustly at all. And if there is [even] the weight of a mustard seed
[…] every soul see what it sends on before it for the day of account
[…][70]

Like the Socratic dictum "an unexamined life is not worth living" by
questioning one's past actions, the dramatic crescendo before entering
the mosque continues as the observer takes steps towards its interior.
The release of tension, through the use of the two floral panels on
either side, however, provides the observer with comfort, thus, easing
any anxiety and suggesting that there may be hope and salvation
ahead. Once inside, however, the self-examination of one's life
becomes even more intense in the midst of thousands of tiles. It is at
the moment for the observer, that the common theme used by Sinan
and Michelangelo can be summed up by Wallace, who writes: "Before
the *Last Judgment* we are made painfully aware of our sins but also
reminded that salvation and the resurrection of the body are still
attainable."[71] That is, for the Christians it is through the Second
Coming of Christ, and for the Muslims it is through their total submission to His Will.

Like Sinan's sacred space, Michelangelo's work also provides an 'uninterrupted view' of the Last Judgement, and of hope and salvation interplaying with the natural and constructed realities of the Last Day. Similarly, by denying the viewer of an exterior view they are forced into contemplation and reflection within the sacred space, and their own spiritual reality as it relates to the message of the fresco. Therefore, the spiritual transformation induced by each of these artworks requires the observer's self-examination. In fact, from the moment one walks into these sacred spaces, one feels compelled to rotate a full 360 degrees so as to take in the engulfing beauty. The 'revolving' of the observer can be likened to the Sufi *sema* ceremony, where whirling dervishes become one with God, or to pilgrimage (*hajj*) to Mecca and circumambulation of the Kaba. It may even be considered to be like the motion of the planets that orbit our sun, but ultimately it is an act in which one can shed all their worldly desires and seek His forgiveness and mercy, as both artworks encourage one to do. According to Rumi, "whirling is the business of the spirit that cannot stay in one place."[72] The 'whirling experience' is "a piece of the heart; a connection to God and a hope of finding the Beloved. When we listen to those beautiful sounds, the imagination in our hearts strengthens; those imaginings even take on forms from breath."[73] In other words, by entering the state of spiritual ecstasy that comes through 'whirling', one's love of God is enhanced and vices of the heart are washed away, thus, saving the dervish from himself and bringing him spiritually closer to the Divine. According to Richard Etlin, the 'whirling' space becomes,

[...] an integral constituent of the self [...] Our aesthetic response to scenes of nature and to works of art, to their qualities of line, from, and mass, is a composite sentiment that involves a bodily sense of self, which also has its spatial dimension. At the deepest end of the aesthetic scale, in situations to which we attach the notion of the sublime, it is the spatial sense of self that is most directly engaged in a pantheistic feeling of transport and transcendence.[74]

In both Michelangelo's *Last Judgement* and Sinan's *çini* aesthetics of the Rustem Pasha Mosque, one feels that their world is not so distant from the Divine, and is lifted into the spiritual world that is presented in front of, and above, them. As Patricia Trutty-Coohill explains of her experience at the Sistine Chapel: "[w]hile the world was above me, it was not beyond me. I recognized the sense of that world because it was an extension of my own. It transcended the room, yet was also immanent."[75] Much like attaining a transcendental state through the act of whirling one can also find God through the influence of the art, like a moth that is drawn to the light. In such a spiritual state even personal salvation becomes de-emphasised, as the only thing that matters in such a moment is union with the One. Rumi elaborated on this idea, which, while many years before Hall's time, are consistent with her interpretation of the resurrection of the body portrayed in the *Last Judgement* and the allusion of paradise created by Sinan:

It was clapping hands because it escaped death and was dancing in the air like the branches and leaves of trees. When the branches and the leaves come out of the prisonof soil they raise their heads above the ground and become friends with the wind and start to dance with it [...] They dance to the tune of love and attain perfection as the moon [...] Their bodies move and dance. But in what state are their spirits? [...] There is no way to explain them.[76]

Unable to explain the state of the souls after death, Rumi considered the dancing of the figures resurrected from their graves and saved from death, as the first stage of salvation. Similarly, such 'dancing' is alluded to in Michelangelo's fresco as shown by the twisted bodies that are rising toward their heavenly destination. This depiction echoes the words of Rumi, insofar as the figures have "escaped death and [dance] in the air like the branches and leaves of trees."[77] Sinan's abstraction of the floral images displayed on Iznik tiles, which become more intense in the *mihrab* panels, also resonates with Rumi's couplets (above). Here, the observer, standing in front of the *mihrab* after entering the sacred space, may feel his/her spirit to be like leaves breaking out of the buds on branches as they climb up the metaphorical tree of Paradise. However, because these two art media are earthly representations of salvation and Paradise, there still remain questions of uncertainty related to what happens to the spirit, which even Rumi could not explain. This uncertainty reinforces the angst that is displayed in the *Last Judgement* and the conscious of the observer in the Rustem Pasha Mosque. It can be argued that both artworks achieve their intended purpose in stimulating the metaphysical anxiety in the observer. As Franz Marc explains, the goal of art was "to reveal unearthly life dwelling behind everything, to break the mirror of life so that we may look being in the face."[78] From a Jungian perspective, by looking at the self in the face raises conscious awareness and experience in creating a new pattern of life encouraging inner growth.

Aesthetics of Michelangelo and Sinan: The act of Judgement

As Michelangelo aged and began struggling with his mortality, his poetry and use of biblical passages suggest that he suffered from his spirit and his flesh working in opposition to each other. As noted above, this tension had been a theological idea that troubled Christianity since its beginnings, and was also manifested in Michelangelo's fresco. The salvation of the spirit from the mortality of the flesh can be seen in the words of Saint Paul, Romans 7: "What a wretched man I am. Who will save me from this body doomed to die? Thanks be to Jesus Christ, our Lord and God, who frees us from this world". In this passage from Matthew 25[79] the Lord desires holiness as much as the spirit, while the body becomes the oppressor, and through this lens one can also see the *Last Judgement's* expression that the flesh and the sins that it carries "twist us, set us off balance like [Michelangelo's] figures' *contrapposto*" *(Figure 16).*[80] This is also seen in Giovanni di Paolo's fifteenth century representation of Dante's souls of the damned in Hell *(Figure 16a).*

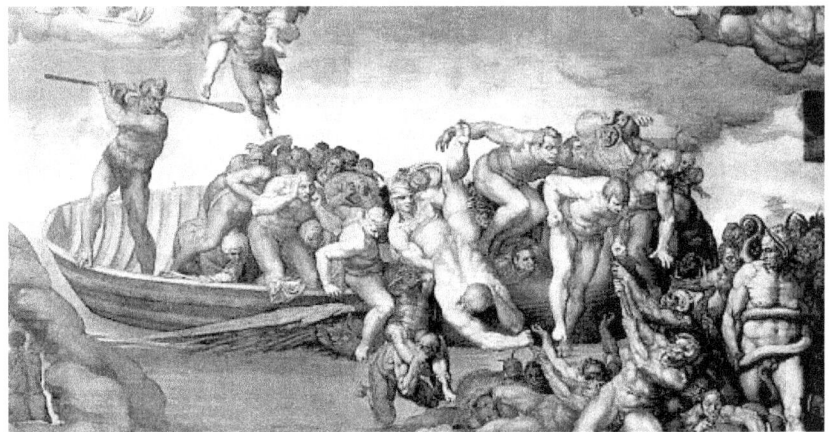

Figure 16. Photograph of the detail from the 'Last Judgement' depicting Charon the boatman taking the lost souls into hell. Photograph reproduction.

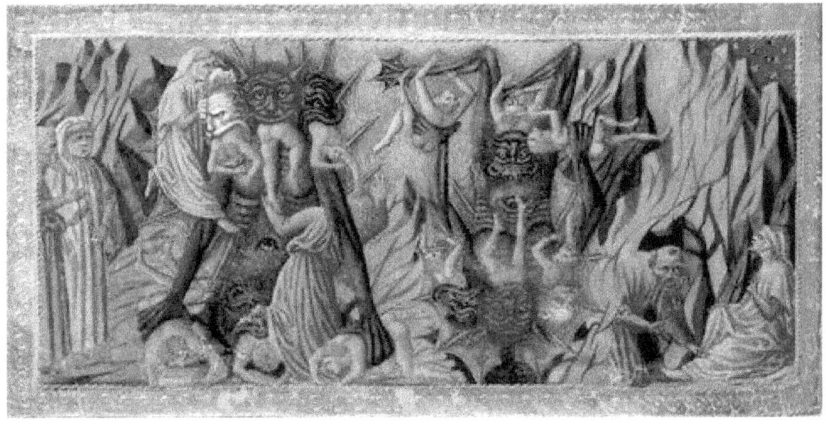

Figure 16a. Dante and Beatrice in Hell witnessing the suffering of the souls of the damned. Giovanni di Paolo, c.1444-1452. British Library. Photograph reproduction.

Like Mir Heidar's representation of Muhammad visiting Hell and witnessing the suffering of the sinners in Figure 9f above, so too does Giovanni di Paolo's version of the underworld and Michelangelo's *Last Judgement* representation of the damned souls inspired by Dante's *Divine Comedy* become one of the significant features in the Christian ascension narrative of the Renaissance.

According to de Tolnay, Michelangelo's innovation to create something new broke with tradition. For example, he disregarded the traditional use of uniform perspective in favour of a shifting perspective in which each group of figures appears in its own self-contained space. The figures at the top of the wall are larger than those at the bottom, which is in complete contrast to what would be expected of traditional perspective. However, in doing so, Michelangelo ensured "consistency of intensity throughout the fresco" when viewed from floor level.[81] Additionally, by having the altar wall slope—by extending the top by 28 centimetres further than the bottom—he brought the Last Day alive for the viewer; not in a theological sense, but in an artistic sense.[82] There is also intensity to the *contrapposto* figures of the saints and martyrs, which surround the figure of Christ. By twisting these figures Michelangelo create both angst and relief felt by the individuals preparing for Divine judgement. According to Catholic tradition, saints and martyrs make it to Heaven as a result of their exemplary lives and deaths; in other words, a life of contemplation and service to humanity and God is seen to ensure one's success in the afterlife. Therefore, the figures who surround the Christ figure are mainly saints and martyrs who had violent deaths, and signify the heroes of the Christian faith. Using the face of Pope Paul III to model the face of Peter[83] unites the papacy as the successors of Peter, from whom their spiritual authority derived. Additionally, there is a look of agitation on each of their faces —no one is traveling peacefully into Heaven—and there is dramatic tension around the figure of Christ. To an observer of the fresco, which this may seem harsh, "in depicting the martyrs holding out symbols of their death, calling for salvation, Michelangelo is firmly coming down on the side of justice, perhaps even Divine retribution, for the martyrs in this instance are demanding recompense."[84]

The decision to place the altar wall in a direction facing the sun was deliberately done in order to symbolically face the 'direction of death'. According to Connor, "[t]he fresco seems appropriate for that western wall and the setting of the sun because it depicts the end of the world [...] the death of the universe, in which all actions and thoughts of the human race are summed up in the division between the elect and the damned.".[85] Marcia Hall, however, disagrees. In considering the theme of judgement, Hall believes Michelangelo actually "de-emphasized" it in his fresco: "[h]e has eliminated the act of judgement [and] the Weighing of the Souls."[86] By doing so the Last Judgement thus rests in our hands and we become the masters of our destiny both in this life and the next reinforcing Condivi's words when he comments on the angel holding the Book of Life, "...everyone reads and recognises his past life, having almost judged himself."[87]

Sinan de-emphasised the act of judgement in the interior of his mosque. When entering the mosque the sheer brilliance of the tiles stands out as one large painting, alluding to God's promised Paradise. Unlike Catholicism, in Islam, one needs no intermediaries to achieve salvation. From the entrance to the mosque two large floral panels, much like Renaissance paintings, which welcome the believer to God's promised kingdom, greet the individual. The interior aesthetics created by the Iznik tiles, depicting over 80 different floral styles, represent an image of Paradise as promised in the Qur'an and echoes the depictions of heaven from the *Mi'raj-name* manuscripts in Figures 9a-c and 9e above. The soothing effect of the sea of cobalt blue, which engulfs one upon entry to the mosque, creates a sense of elation and spiritual uplifting and weightlessness. Similarly, Michelangelo's fresco, which dominates the altar of the Sistine Chapel, shows the figure of Christ as the saviour of humanity and bears hope for the righteous with its use of a bright blue background—signifying the dawning of a new age and new beginning with the Second Coming. The *qibla* wall of the Rustem Pasha Mosque can also be seen as an altar wall, and faces the direction of the Kaba *(Figures 17, 18)*. This reminds one that any hope of salvation can only exist in His presence. However, the mosque also reminds the believer that achieving salvation will not be easy. The back-lit, stained-glass windows of the artist Ibrahim "punctuate the *qibla* wall" and make the tiles look "dark and shadowy."[88] Additionally, the frugal use of red on the *qibla* wall creates a similar effect; symbolising the obstacles along one's journey to Paradise, such as having to answer for one's actions on earth. Denny's criticism of this design decision is that the tile decorations are lost in the huge interior of the mosque.[89] This feeling of loss and uncertainty suggested by Denny, from an Islamic perspective, was likely done to remind the believer of the incomprehensibility of the Divine by the human mind.

Unlike Dante's anthropomorphising God as the human incarnate in Christ in the *Divine Comedy* and vividly articulated in Michelangelo's *Last Judgement*, the Islamic tradition's vehement and unequivocal opposition to this act expressed in the Qur'an and Prophet Muhammad's *mir'aj* experience proclaims a more abstract and incorporeal approach to understanding the Divine (*Figures 19, 20*). Despite this divergent approach in the representation of Divine Judgement, in both Michelangelo's and Sinan's sacred spaces, the artists achieve intense emotional mediums where the fundamental notions of earthly experiences are subsumed by the omnipotence and mercy of the Almighty. The binary juxtaposition imbued with the act of judgement is accentuated by the forceful figure of Christ in Figures 18 and 19 with his right hand raised in readiness to pass judgement. Michelangelo's representation of Christ as the Saviour complements God's omniscience with the paradisiacal representations inside the *mihrab* with Iznik *çini* tiles in Figure 20 revealing before our eyes the hope of entering Paradise through the mesmerising effect of the floral ensemble of the tiles. Furthermore, theologically speaking, as Michelangelo succeeds in articulating the Christian doctrine of Christ as the Saviour figure in the *Last Judgement* fresco, Sinan, similarly triumphs in his visual vocabulary the Islamic belief in the *tawhid* and *ittihad* through the abstract naturalism of the Iznik *çini*.

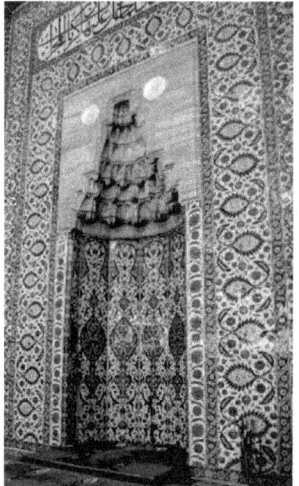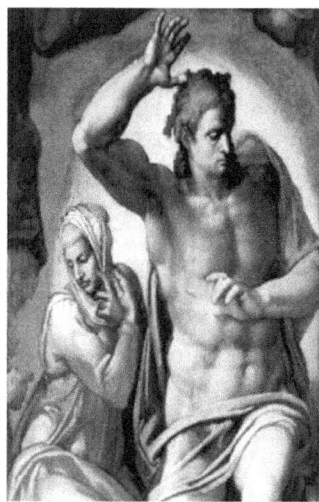

Figures 17, 18. Left, detail of the mihrab wall. The frame around the mihrab niche consists of tiles that use repeated designs. Some of these design patterns were never repeated in later Iznik tilework, such as the 'stippled' saz leaves that overlap and appear to move; dragon-like, as if blown by a strong wind. Photograph by Metin Mustafa, December 13, 2015; right, photograph of the detail of the Christ figure in the 'Last Judgement'. Photograph reproduction.

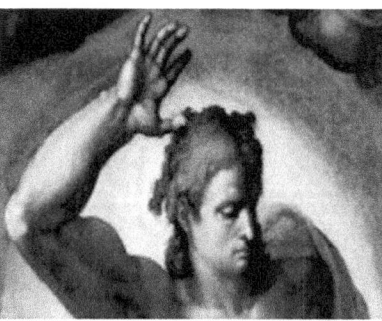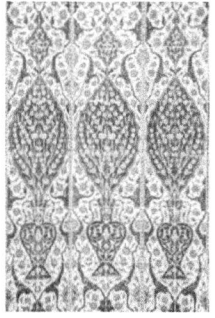

Figures 19, 20. Left, the forceful Christ figure with his right hand raised ready to pass judgement on the dammed souls; right, the mesmerising effect of the floral ensemble of the interior of the mihrab representing the Garden of Eden and the incomprehensibility of God by the human mind. Photograph reproductions.

Aesthetics of Michelangelo and Sinan: Predestination

The doctrine of predestination that is reflected in the *Last Judgement* and the Rustem Pasha Mosque unites the two artworks. Unlike the bearded elderly man who stretches his arm out to Adam in the *Creation of Adam* fresco on the ceiling of the Sistine Chapel (which was Michelangelo's first anthropomorphic God), viewers of the *Last Judgement* become fixated on a specific image of the Divine, i.e., the youthful Christ. Michelangelo's portrayal of Christ is neither 'angry' nor 'vengeful'. Rather, Christ is presented as a figure who assists the resurrected bodies of both the saved and damned, whose actions have already been predetermined in the Book. Hall believes that, despite not being explicitly presented in the fresco, this motif is indeed a part of the work. Furthermore, she rejects the evidence that has been offered by other scholars, who often cite Matthew 24:29-31 or 25:31ff, of a vengeful angry Christ where the Son of Man will descend to earth from Heaven "and he will separate the people from one another as a shepherd separates the sheep from the goats. He will put the sheep on his right and the goats on his left".[90] Hall's anagogical reading of the *Last Judgement*, however, suggests that the actions of Christ, as represented by Michelangelo, is exemplified in 1 Thess. 4:16-17, where Paul says: "the Lord himself will descend from the heaven with a cry of command, with the archangel's call and with the sound of the trumpet of God. And the dead in Christ will rise first; then we who are alive, who are left, shall be caught up together with them in the clouds to meet the Lord in the air" seen in Figure 21. This coincides with Anastasis (Greek Bible) or 'Harrowing of Hell' motif from Greek orthodox iconography in which after death, Christ descends to limbo and retrieves all the souls of the dead, which have not yet seen God, and takes them up to heaven. According to Hall, it is this process that is depicted in the lower part of the *Last Judgement*.[91] In this section of the fresco, where bodies are shown in the beginning of their rise from their graves, some ascend upwards and are assisted by angels while others are pulled down by devils, into an adjacent pit. The angel in the centre who holds the Book of Life oversees the unfolding scenario seen in Figure 22. By leaning forward "attentively [...] it is he, not Christ, who announces the outcome, for the decision has long being made when the name was written, or excluded from the book."[92] Thus, according to Hall, the emphasis here is not on damnation and burning in Hell—as seen in Matthew 25:41 where there is "eternal fire prepared for the devil and his angels"—but rather on the Pauline belief of hope, which is expressed in his doctrine of predestination and states that when one is presented with their Book on the Day, they will recognise their past and almost act as their own judge. Using this interpretation one can see that Michelangelo subverted the 'vengeful and angry Christ' by opting to present the version of Christ who "initiates the flow of movement with an imperious but not condemning nature" (*Figures 21, 22*).[93]

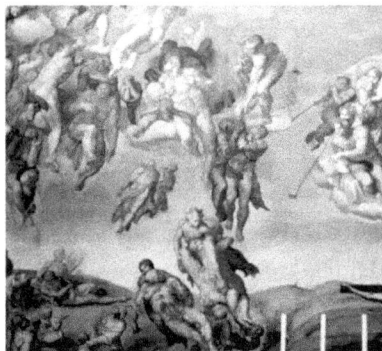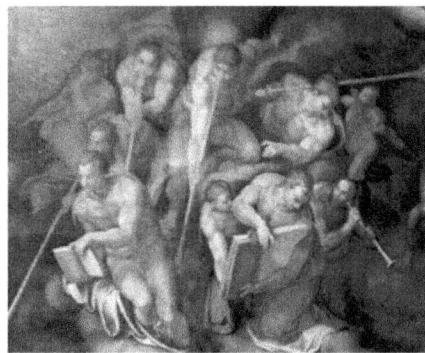

Figures 21, 22. Left, detail of the rising of the souls of the dead from their graves; right, detail of the Sounding of the Trumpet by the archangels signifying the beginning of the Day of Judgement, while the angel in the lower right corner holds the Book of Deeds ready to present to the rising souls their recorded actions on earth prior to meeting their Lord. Photograph reproductions.

Additionally, Qur'anic verses are also consistent with Hall's interpretation of Michelangelo's *Last Judgement* and who is ultimately in control of our final destiny. Just as the actions of the naked figures have been written in the Book held by the angel, who holds their fates in his hand, the Qur'an echoes a similar message in verses 69:19, 25-31: "Then he that will be given his Record in his right hand will say: 'Ah here! Read ye my Record! [...] And he that will be given his Record in his left hand will say: 'Ah! Would that my Record had not been given to me! And that I had never realised how my account (stood)! Ah!

Would that (Death) had made an end of me! Of no profit to me has been my wealth! My power has perished from me!'" Moreover, the ideas of predestination and salvation in the hereafter are further rein-forced by the Qur'anic inscriptions on the white-on-blue lunette tiles surrounding the windows and doors of the upper galleries of the Rustem Pasha Mosque. Not only do the invocations plead for safety from Hell Fire they also plead for support and mercy in this world and the next: "Thou art my Protecting Friend in the world and the Here-after. Make me die submissive (unto Thee), and join me to the right-eous (12:101)." Another invocation repeats the plea by asking for God's favour in both worlds: "Our Lord! Give unto us in the world that which is good and in the Hereafter that which is good, and guard us from the doom of Fire (2:201)." With this in mind, the idea of jour-neying to the next world and the promise of a new life, in whatever state that may be, are predestined by God and confirmed by the Qur'anic inscriptions in the mosque decorative aesthetics acting as reminders of this assurance. Furthermore, one's presence in the sacred space is an affirmation of this belief.

While human representations of God do not occur in Sinan's art, the Islamic notion of predestination is nonetheless exemplified in the architectural feature of the mosque – the *mihrab*. The paradox of free will and predestination is related in the following Qur'anic verses:

Whatever good happens to thee is from God; and whatever evil befalls thee is from thyself [...] Indeed, all things We created with predestination ... If your Lord had so willed all who are on the earth would surely have believed, all of them [...] Indeed, all things We created with predestination.[94]

Although God informs people it is through their choices that evil things befall them, He also reminds Man that not only one's life and death have been predestined, but also that they are only made possible by God's will and are beyond his control. Rumi illustrates this point in the following words:

> We should not tie the evil that comes to us by God's predetermina-
> tion to destiny, but we should maintain comportment and blame
> our self for not using our choice and power to remove the evil in
> us and restrain our self, which dictates evil.[95]

Concurring with the Qur'an, Rumi also acknowledges that evil comes
to us by our own doings. He informs that one should only blame the
self and reflect on one's own actions in order to attain enlightenment.[96]
The individual may believe that it is through his own free will that he
stands before the Almighty in the sacred space represented by the
mihrab decorated with paradisiacal symbolisms of the Garden of Eden.
In fact, paradoxically speaking, the desire to seek the Divine, a good
act in itself acknowledged by the Qur'anic verse above, has already
been predestined (*Figures 23, 24*).

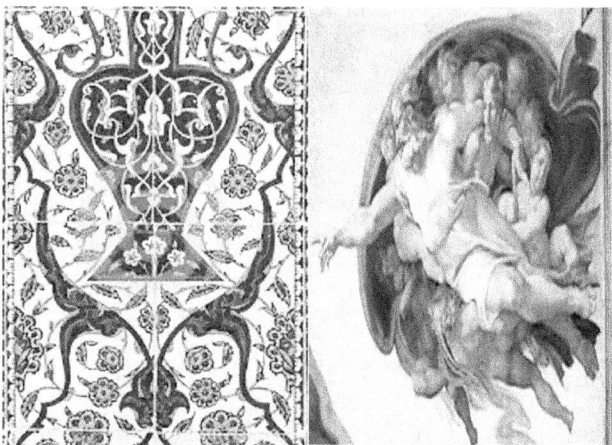

*Figures 23, 24. Left, detail of the mihrab interior displaying the intricate and
elaborate Iznik tile design signifying the duality of the symbolism associated
with this Ottoman art genre the incomprehensibility of God by the human
mind and the Garden of Eden; right, detail of Michelangelo's first anthropomorphic representation of God as the bearded old man from the ceiling of the
Sistine Chapel in the Vatican. Photograph reproductions.*

With this in mind, the symbolic significance of the *mihrab* in the mosque becomes even greater for believers and those seeking *ittihad*, union with God. Whether through free will or predestination, the seeker is there inside the sacred space searching for union with the One. In this way Sinan achieves the desired dichotomy – free will–predestination - symbolically attributed to this significant feature of mosque aesthetics.

CONCLUSION

While no evidence to date has come to light substantiating the meeting between Michelangelo and Sinan, it is correct to state that the *Last Judgement* fresco of Michelangelo and Sinan's Iznik *çini* ensemble in the Rustem Pasha Mosque encapsulate the spirit of Renaissance art. Michelangelo's *buon'* fresco, the *Last Judgement* in the Sistine Chapel and Sinan's use of Iznik *çini* interior decorative aesthetics in the Rustem Pasha Mosque thematically converge. The two artworks invite the individual to contemplate his relationship with the Divine and, ponder on his salvation in the hope of attaining Paradise in the after-life. Inspired by their respective religious traditions and stories of ascension of souls into other worldly realms articulated in the New Testament, the Qur'an, Prophet Muhammad's *Isra* and *Mi'raj* experiences, and Dante's *Divine Comedy*, both Michelangelo and Sinan, through the vibrancy of colours, textures, designs and tones, evocatively express the mystical and transcendental narratives in their art works. In sacred spaces the extra sensory perceptions are heightened through the theophanic experience to receive spiritual enlightenment. The heightened sensory perceptions stimulated by the surrounding symbols and colours evoke the otherworldly realm of the *'alam al-mithal'* (Imaginal World) and the 'World of Souls and Lights' (*malakut*) espoused by Ibn Arabi, Rumi and other Sufi masters. Although the strong desire to connect with an omniscient, omnipresent and omnipotent being with the hope of attaining eternal salvation in the Hereafter is very subjective and can never be substantiated, its transformative effect on one's life cannot be questioned either. As Jung argues:

> There is, however, a strong empirical reason why we should cultivate thoughts that can never be proved. It is that they are known to be useful. Man positively needs general ideas and convictions that will give a meaning to his life and enable him to find a place for himself in the universe ... [1]

The Renaissance art of Michelangelo and Sinan provide the powerful visual symbolisms to awaken the spirit and seek something that is much bigger than it.

The art of Michelangelo and Sinan is a spiritual expression of the universe, harmony of colours and forms. Whatever form art expression is manifest, either abstract or geometrical, it possesses an inner dimension, and this is true of Michelangelo's fresco, the *Last Judgement* and Sinan's floral designs of Iznik *çini*. While the Renaissance paved the way for man to broaden his intellectual horizons based on logical thought, religion and religious symbolisms continued to play significant roles in the Catholic Church responding to the Protestant movement sweeping Europe at the time. The fresco responds to the schism in the Church and reinforces the Christian doctrine of the resurrection of the body through the commissioning of Michelangelo's *Last Judgement* during the Counter-Reformation. Politically and symbolically speaking, the fresco serves as a reminder of the unifying message of the Church doctrine and of man's salvation.

Similarly, the Ottomans staged their own distinctive Renaissance in the sixteenth century marking the zenith of their artistic achievements under Sinan, the imperial architect of Süleyman the Magnificent. Like their Christian counterparts in the Latin West, Sinan, deeply ingrained in the mystical interpretation of the Islamic Sufi tradition, set out to create a sacred space through abstract naturalism of Iznik *çini* signifying not only a worldly paradise but also a symbolic representation of the world to come. Using rich vibrant colours including the predominant blue and red to accentuate the floral patterns on thousands of square Iznik tiles, he covered the entire interior of the mosque space. Just as the powerful God-Christ like figure dominate the *Last Judgement* fresco, the symbolic representation of God's omniscience through the variety of tulips against the blue and white in the mosque equally achieves a similar purpose. The result is one of overwhelming spiritual experience stimulating the senses. The combination of the floral ensembles and colours stir the soul and brings it closer to the Divine. In line with the Vasarian definition of the Renaissance, Sinan, like Michelangelo, engaged in the spirit of the age through learning from both the classical past and his inherited Islamic-Ottoman heritage allowing him to adapt, appropriate and innovate. Like Michelangelo's religious artwork emphasising the Christian tradition, Sinan's creation both reinforced and made sense of his place in the faith system of the early modern Ottoman mindset.

The *Last Judgement* fresco of Michelangelo and the Iznik *çini* of Sinan achieve in conveying the mysterious nature of the Divine. From the Sufi humanist and Jungian perspectives, the closer one gets to the Divine, the more incomprehensible He is to the human mind. Ibn Arabi and Jung acknowledge the significance of religious symbols in translating the incomprehensible "Divine" to the human mind. Symbols reinforce the stimulation of human reason to make sense of the mesmerising visual rhetoric, however, as human reason is incapable of ascertaining the incomprehensible, this image simply is identified as "God" or "Allah". According to Jung:

Thus a word or an image is symbolic where it implies something more than its obvious and immediate meaning. It has a wider "unconscious" aspect that is never precisely defined or fully explained. Nor can one hope to define or explain it. As the mind explores the symbol, it is led to ideas that lie beyond the grasp of reason. [Certain symbols] may lead our thoughts toward the concept of a "divine" ... but at this point reason must admit its incompetence; man is unable to define a "divine" being. When, with all our intellectual limitations, we call something "divine". We have merely given it a name, which may be based on a creed, but never on factual evidence. Because there are innumerable things beyond the range of human understanding, we constantly use symbolic terms to represent concepts that we cannot define or fully comprehend. This is one reason why all religions employ symbolic language or images.[2]

Muhammad's prostration before the all-consuming Light of God in Figure 9g is represented in Sinan's tiles in the mesmerising *mihrab* and Michelangelo's all powerful Christ figure whom Dante identified in his vision as one of the three large circles embodying the Holy Trinity in Figure 10b equally underpin the incomprehensibility of the nature of God by the human mind. While God may be incomprehensible to the human mind, salvation and paradise are attainable through His Signs as symbols and as reminders of His Beauty. Hence, the language of religious symbolisms conveyed by the art of Michelangelo and Sinan achieve their intended purpose.

It can therefore be argued that the highly stylised abstract naturalism of Sinan's Iznik *çini* arranged in fresco-like panels to form eschatological and anagogical narratives "is no less powerful in effect as the finger of God touching the finger of Adam in Michelangelo" or the right hand of Christ raised above his head to pass judgement on the rising souls from their graves.[3] This meeting point between Michelangelo and Sinan underscores their achievements in creating anagogical and eschatological works with religious symbolisms capturing their genius as artists of the Renaissance underpinning the *zeitgeist* that epitomised sixteenth century Mediterranean world.

NOTES

INTRODUCTION

1. Gülru Necipoğlu, *The Age of Sinan: Architectural Culture in the Ottoman Empire* (London: Reaktion Books, 2005), 13.
2. Ibid., 13.
3. Carl G. Jung, *Man and his Symbols* (New York: Anchor Press, 1964), 244.
4. Ibid., 245.
5. See the Qur'an, 5:97, 52:4.
6. For more see M. Muhsin Khan, trans. *The Translation of the Meanings of Summarized Sahih Al-Bukhari, Arabic-English* (Karachi: Kazi Publications Inc., 1995).
7. See Khan, *The Translation of the Meanings of Summarized Sahih Al-Bukhari.*
8. For more see A. Guillaume, *The Life of Muhammad: A translation of Ibn Ishaq's Sirat Rasul Allah* (Oxford: Oxford University Press, 1982), 185.
9. Franz Marc cited in Jung, *Man and his Symbols,* 262.
10. 'Contemplation, Constructed Space, and Senses,' YouTube Video, lecture by Phoebe Crisman with an introduction by Kim Tanzer, April 6, 2013, posted by University of Virginia Contemplative Sciences Center, August 19, 2013, accessed May 5, 2015, http://www.youtube.com/watch?v=6FASJrighYE
11. See Sa'i, *Sinan's Autobiographies: Five Sixteenth Century Texts,* Introductory Notes, Critical Editions, and Translations by Howard Crane and Esra Akin, edited by Gülru Necipoğlu (Leiden: Brill, 2006).
12. Ayesha Ramachandran, *The Worldmakers: Global Imagining in Early Modern Europe* (Chicago: The University of Chicago Press, 2015), 7.
13. Jung, *Man and his Symbols,* 89.
14. George L. Raymond, *Art in Theory: An Introduction to the study of comparative aesthetics* (New York: G. T. Putnam Sons, 1894), 76.
15. Michelangelo, *The Complete Poems of Michelangelo,* trans. John Frederick Nims (Chicago: University of Chicago Press, 2000), 63.
16. Sa'i, *Sinan's Autobiographies,* 53, 64.
17. Ibid., 65.
18. Ibid., 66.

I. THE RENAISSANCE AND THE MEDITERRANEAN ZEITGEIST

1. Gülru Necipoğlu, *The Age of Sinan,* 13. For more on Ottoman Renaissance see Metin Mustafa, *The Ottoman Renaissance: A Reconsideration of Early Modern Ottoman Art, 1413-1575* (New Jersey: Blue Dome Press, 2019). On the architecture and aesthetics of Sinan also see Gülru Necipoğlu, 'Challenging the Past: Sinan and the Competitive Discourse of Early Modern Islamic Architecture,' *Muqarnas* vol. 10 (Leiden: Brill, 1993): 169–180, accessed April 24, 2015, http://www.jstor.org/stable/1523183?

seq=1#page_scan_tab_contents; Gülru Necipoğlu, 'Creation of a National Genius: Sinan and the Historiography of 'Classical' Ottoman Architecture,' *Muqarnas* vol. 24 (Leiden: Brill, 2006), accessed April 24, 2015, http://isites.harvard.edu/fs/docs/icb.topic570061.files//articles/Creation_Genius.pdf

2. The book will refer to both electronic and hard copies of Vasari's Lives. Giorgio Vasari, *The Lives of the Painters, Sculptors and Architects*, trans. Gaston Du C. de Vere, 10 vols. (London: Macmillan & Co. Ld. & The Medici Society, LD, 1912-14) http://members.efn.org/~acd/vite/VasariLives.html; Giorgio Vasari, *The Lives of the Painters, Sculptors and Architects, trans.* Jonathan Foster (New York: Dover Publications, 2005), Kindle; for book publication, Giorgio Vasari, *The Lives of the Painters, Sculptors and Architects*, ed. William Gaunt, 4 vols. (New York: Dent, 1963).

3. For more see E. H. Gombrich, "The Renaissance Conception of Artistic Progress and its Consequences," in *Norm and Form: Studies in the Art of the Renaissance* (London: Phaidon Press, 1966), 1-10.

4. "…della loro perfezione e rovina e restaurazione e per dir meglio rinascita…," Giorgio Vasari, *Le vite de' piu eccellenti pittori, scultori ed architetti* (Torino: Letteratura italiana Einaudi, 1986), 125, http://www.letteraturaitaliana.net/pdf/Volume_5/t129.pdf. For English translation see Vasari, *Preface to Part I, The Lives*, accessed May 5, 2016, http://members.efn.org/~acd/vite/VasariPreface.html

5. Vasari, *Preface to Part II, The Lives*, accessed May 5, 2016, http://members.efn.org/~acd/vite/VasariPreface2.html

6. Vasari, *Part III of The Lives*.

7. For more see Hans Baron, *The Crisis of the Early Italian Renaissance* (Princeton: Princeton University Press, 1966).

8. Vasari, *Preface to The Lives*.

9. "…lavorata di mano d'Andrea Taffi con la medesima maniera greca, ma invero molto piú bella …" Giorgio Vasari, Le vite de' piu eccellenti architetti pittori, et scultori italiani da Cimabue insino a'tempi nostri (Firenze: Torentino, 1550), http://bepi1949.altervista.org/vasari/vasari10.htm

10. Vasari, *Part I of The Lives*, accessed May 5, 2016, http://members.efn.org/~acd/vite/VasariGioPisano.htm1

11. Vasari, *Part I of The Lives*, http://members.efn.org/~acd/vite/VasariGioPisano.htm1

12. Vasari, *Part III of The Lives*, accessed May 5, 2016, http://members.efn.org/~acd/vite/VasariMichelangelo7.html

13. Lee Sanstead, "The Meaning of Michelangelo's David" (5 September 2004), accessed February 19, 2017, http://www.sandstead.com/essays/david.html

14. Vasari, *Part III of The Lives*, http://members.efn.org/~acd/vite/VasariMichelangelo3.html

15. Ibid.

16. Vasari, *Preface to The Lives*.

17. See Ulrich Libbrecht, "Comparative Philosophy: A Methodological Approach," in *Worldviews and Cultures: Philosophical Reflections from an Intercultural Perspective*, ed. Nicole Note et al. (Brussels: Springer, 2009).

18. Libbrecht, "Comparative Philosophy," 34.

19. Vasari, *Preface to The Lives*.

20. Ibid.

21. Also see Alexander Nagel and Christopher Wood, "Towards a New Model of Renaissance Anachronism," *Art Bulletin* 87 (2005): 408.

22. Walter B. Denny, *Iznik: The Artistry of Ottoman Ceramics* (London: Thames and London, reprinted 2010), 18.
23. Leibniz in T. Hentsch, *Imagining the Middle East* (Montreal: Black Rose Books, 1992), 96.
24. James R. Lehning, *To be a Citizen: The Political Culture of the Early French Third Republic* (London: Cornell University Press, 2001), 132.
25. For more see P. Murray and L. Murray, *The Art of the Renaissance* (London, Thames and London) 1963, 9; Jerry Brotton, *The Renaissance Bazaar: From the Silk Road to Michelangelo* (New York: Oxford University Press, 2002), Kindle. Kindle edition, 21–22; also see Jacob Burckhardt, *The Civilisation of the Renaissance in Italy* (Pisa: Aonia edizioni, 2011).
26. Michelet, cited in Brotton, *The Renaissance Bazaar,* Loc.254.
27. Ibid., Loc.260.
28. Burckhardt, *The Civilisation of the Renaissance in Italy*, 9.
29. W. K. Ferguson, *The Renaissance in Historical Thought* (Cambridge, MA: Houghton Mifflin Company, 1948), 222-223, 240-243.
30. Ferguson, *The Renaissance in Historical Thought*, 28; M. L. McLaughlin, 'Humanist Concept of Renaissance and Middle Ages in the Tre- and Quattrocento,' *Renaissance Studies* 2 (1988): ix, 131-42.
31. For more see Arthur Hughes, 'Interpreting the Renaissance,' *Oxford Art Journal* 11 (1988): 77-78.
32. Edward Said, *Orientalism* (London: Penguin Books, 1995), 7.
33. Erwin Panofsky, *Renaissance and Renascences in Western Art* (Almqvist & Wiksell, 1969), 38.
34. Brotton, *The Renaissance Bazaar,* Loc. 364.
35. Said, *Orientalism*, 342-343.
36. Z. Sardar, *Orientalism* (Buckingham: Open University Press, 1999), vii.
37. Ibid., 31.
38. Claire Norton, 'Blurring the Boundaries: Intellectual and Cultural Interactions between Eastern and Western: Christian and Muslim Worlds', in *The Renaissance and the Ottoman World,* edited by Anna Contadini and Claire Norton (England: Ashgate Publishing Limited, 2013), 3.
39. See Homi Bhabha, *The Location of Cultures* (London & New York: Routledge, 1994), Kindle edition.
40. Stuart Hill, 'The Spectacle of the 'Other'', in *Representation: Cultural Representations and Signifying Practices,* edited by Stuart Hill (London: Sage Publications, 2003), 261.
41. Ibid., 271.
42. Gerald MacClean, 'Introduction: Re-Orienting the Renaissance', in *Re-Orienting the Renaissance: Cultural Exchanges With the East,* ed., Gerald MacClean (New York: Palgrave Macmillan, 2005), 8. For more on revisionist historiography see D. J. Castellano's essay on 'The Renaissance Concept of Self as seen in Petrarch, Castiglione and Montaigne,' (Massachusetts: Boston University, 2002), accessed May 23, 2016, http://www.arcaneknowledge.org/histschol/renaissance.htm
43. Jardine and Brotton, *Global Interest,* 61.
44. Ibid., 61.
45. Ibid., 61.
46. Lisa Jardine, *Worldly Goods: A New History of the Renaissance* (New York: W. W. Norton & Company, Inc., 1996), back cover.
47. Ibid., xi.

48. See Jerry Brotton, *The Renaissance: A Very Short Introduction* (New York: Oxford University Press, 2006), 8; also see Matteo Burioni, 'Vasari's Rinascita: History, Anthropology or Art Criticism,' accessed January 29, 2016, https://www.academia.edu/2638258/Vasari_s_rinascita._History_anthropology_or_art_criticis, 117.

49. Rosamond E. Mack, *Bazaar to Piazza: Islamic Trade and Italian Art, 1300-1600* (Berkeley: University of California, 2002), 179.

50. Friedrich Adler, 'Die Moscheen zu Constantinopel: Eine architektonische baugeschictliche Studie,' (The Mosques of Constantinople: An Architectural Study), *Deutsche Bauzeitung* 8 (1874): 65–66, 73–76, 81–83, 89–91, 97– 99.

51. See Corneilus Gurlitt, *Istanbul'un Mimari Sanatı, Architecture of Constantinople, Die Baukunst Konstantinopels* translated by Rezan Kæzæltan (Ankara: Enformasyon ve Dokumantasyon Hizmetleri Vakfı, 1999), 59, 66, 96. The work has been translated from Cornelius Gurlitt, *Die Baukunst Konstantinopels*, 2 vols. (Berlin: 1907).

52. Ibid., 96.

53. See Franz Babinger, 'Die türkische Renaissance: Bemerkungen zum Schaffen des grossen türkischen Baumeisters Sinân,' *Beiträge zur Kenntnis des Orients* 9 (1914): 67–88.

54. Franz Babinger, 'Ein osmanischer Michelangelo,' *Frankfurter Zeitung*, Sept. 7, 1915, no. 248.

55. Ernst Diez, *Türk Sanatı: Başlangıcından Günümüze Kadar*, trans. Oktay Aslanapa, (Istanbul, 1946), 232.

56. Ibid., 232.

57. Ibid., 6–7, 27, 138–39, 170, 192–98. Also see Halil Inalcık, *The Ottoman Empire: The Classical Age 1300–1600*, (London: Butler & Tanner, 1973).

58. Esin Atıl, *Süleymanname: The Illustrated History of Süleyman the Magnificent* (Washington: National Gallery of Art, 1986), 31. Also see *The Age of Süleyman the Magnificent* (NSW, Australia: Art Exhibitions Australia / Beagle Press, 1990, Exhibition Publication); Esin Atıl, 'The Image of Süleyman in Ottoman Art,' in *Süleyman the Second and His Time*, edited by Halil Inalcik and Cemal Kafadar (Istanbul: The Isis Press, 2010), 333–341.

59. Doğan Kuban, *Ottoman Architecture* (Suffolk, UK: Antique Collectors Club Distributors, 2010), 246-247.

60. 'Interview with Gülru Necipoğlu,' by Gizem Tongo, Department of History at Bogaziçi University, Istanbul, August 2009, accessed August 15, 2017, http://isites.harvard.edu/fs/docs/icb.topic732589.files//Gizem_Tongo_Interview-GULRU_NECIPOGLU.pdf

61. Godfrey Goodwin, *A History of Ottoman Architecture* (London, UK: Thames and Hudson, 1971), 6.

62. Denny, *Iznik: The Artistry of Ottoman Ceramics*, 22.

63. See Nurhan Atasoy and Julian Raby. *Iznik: The Pottery of Ottoman Turkey*, edited by Yanni Petsopoulos (London: Thames and Hudson, 1989), 14-49; also see Atıl, *Süleymanname*, 31-35.

64. Nancy Bisaha, *Creating East and West: Renaissance Humanists and the Ottoman Turks* (Philadelphia: University of Pennsylvania Press, 2006), 174.

65. Ibid., 174.

66. James Hankins, 'Renaissance Crusaders: Humanist Crusade Literature in the Age of Mehmed II,' in *Dumbarton Oaks Papers*, Vol. 49, Symposium on Byzantium and the Italians, 13th-15th Centuries (1995): 111-207. Also see Thierry Hentsch, *Imagining the Middle East*, 165; Paul Coles, *Ottoman Impact on Europe* (Harcourt: Brace & World, 1968), 12; Bernard Lewis, *Islam and the West* (London: Oxford University Press, 1993).

67. S. Yerasimos, *Constantinople: Istanbul's Historical Heritage* (Paris: H. F. Ullmann Publishing, 2012), 276. Also see Henry Matthews, 'Rethinking Ottoman Architecture.' Paper presented at the ACSA International Conference, 2001; Brian Sewell, 'Sinan: The Architect of a Forgotten Renaissance,' *Cornucopia*, 1992/93.

68. Selda Besnier- Kılıçioğlu, 'Sinan and Palladio: The Parallel Development of Two Master-Builders,' *The UNESCO Courier: a window open on the world* XLI, no. 3 (1988), accessed March 4, 2014, http://unesdoc.unesco.org/images/0007/000781/078126eo.pdf#77905, p.34.

69. Guido Ruggiero, ed., *A Companion to the Worlds of the Renaissance* (Malden: MA: Blackwell Publishing, 200), 3.

70. Necipoğlu, *The Age of Sinan*,13, 15.

71. D. Soyini Madison, *Critical Ethnography: Method, Ethics, and Performance* (Los Angeles: Sage Publications, 2012), 58.

72. Ibid., 58.

73. Sa'i, *Sinan's Autobiographies*, 130.

74. "...bu şerh ü tafsili sahayıf-ı rüzgârda nümüne ü yādgār kalmak içün." See Sa'i, *Sinan's Autobiographies*, 62, 59.

75. "her küngüre-'i eyvāndan bir gūşe ve her zāviye-'i virāndan bir tūşe peydā eyleyūp ..." See Sa'i, *Sinan's Autobiographies*, 115, 142.

76. Sa'i, *Sinan's Autobiographies*, 74, 85, 156.

77. Ibid., 65, 75, 85. For definitions of Ottoman-Turkish words see *Yeni Cep Lügat.*

78. "günden güne envā'-i 'imaretler ihtira' olınup nezāket izdiyād bulmışdur ..." See Sa'i, *Sinan's Autobiographies*, 65, 78, 131.

79. Ibid., 74-5.

80. Ibid., 74.

81. Ibid., 123.

82. See Vasari, *Preface to Part I, The Lives.*

83. Sa'i, *Sinan's Autobiographies*, 123, 131.

84. Selen B. Morkoç, "Reading Architecture from the Text: The Ottoman Story of the Four Marble Columns," accessed February 9, 2018. https://www.academia.edu/27608699/Reading_Architecture_from_Text_The_Story_of_the_Four_Marble_Columns, 34.

85. Sa'i, *Sinan's Autobiographies*, 122.

86. Spiro Kostof, *A History of Architecture: Settings and Rituals* (New York: Oxford University Press, 1985), 459.

87. Necipoğlu, *The Age of Sinan*, 13-23.

88. Henry A. Milton and Craig Hugh Smyth, *Michelangelo Architect: The Façade of San Lorenzo and the Drum of the Dome of St. Peter's* (Milan: Olivetti, 1988), 102. Also see Joseph Connors, 'Borromini, Hagia Sophia, and S. Vitale', in *Architectural Studies in Memory of Richard Krautheimer*, ed. Cecil Striker (Mainz: Verlag Philipp Von Zabern, 1996), 43-48.

89. For the building of the Süleymaniye Mosque dates see Sa'i, *Sinan's Autobiographies*.

90. For St. Peter's see F. Hartt, *History of Italian Renaissance Art* (6th ed.) (Englewood Cliffs: Prentice Hall, 2006).

91. See Connors, 'Borromini, Hagia Sophia, and S. Vitale', 43-48.

92. Ibid., 45.

93. For more on this, see Henry A. Milton and V. Lampugnani, eds. *The Renaissance from Brunelleschi to Michelangelo: The Representation of Architecture* (Milan: Rizzoli, 1994), 612, 645, 658-64.

94. See Jean-Claude Flachat, 1766, cited in Necipoğlu, *The Age of Sinan*, 102.

95. Francesco Dei Marchi, cited in Necipoğlu, *The Age of Sinan*, 101.

96. See Howard Burns, "Building and Construction in Palladio's Vicenza" in *Les Chantiers de la renaissance*, ed. A. Chastel and J. Guillaume (Paris: Piccard, 1991), 191-226.

97. See Morkoc, "An Architect to Challenge Them All," 15; also see Necipoğlu, *The Age of Sinan*, 13, 15.

98. David Lowenthal, *The Past is a Foreign Country* (Cambridge: Cambridge University Press, 1985), 339.

99. Gülru Necipoğlu-Kafadar, "The Süleymaniye Complex in Istanbul: An Interpretation," *Muqarnas 3* (1985): 92-117, accessed February 19, 2015, 2018http://www.jstor.org/stable/1523086?origin=JSTOR-pdf, 92.

100. Rüsen, Jörn. "What is Historical Consciousness? - A Theoretical Approach to Empirical Evidence," translated by Wolfgang Gebhard. Paper presented at Canadian Historical Consciousness in an International Context: Theoretical Frameworks, University of British Columbia, Vancouver, BC, 2001, 4.

101. Vasari, *Preface to Part I, The Lives.*

102. See Vasari, *Part III of The Lives,* http://members.efn.org/~acd/vite/VasariMichelangelo8.html; and Sa'i, *Sinan's Autobiographies*, 74-75.

103. Aristotle, "Nicomachean Ethics", Book IV, accessed March 22, 2015, http://www.sacred-texts.com/cla/ari/nico/nico036.htm

2. SUFI HUMANISM AND ISLAMIC ART

1. Seyyed Hossein Nasr, *Islamic Art and Spirituality* (New York: State University of New York Press, 1987), ix.

2. See David P. Brewster, 'The Study of Sufism: Towards a methodology,' accessed June 24, 2017, https://www.sciencedirect.com/sdfe/pdf/download/eid/1-s2.0-0048721X76900476/first-page-pdf, 31.

3. Ibid., 31.

4. Nasr, *Islamic Art and Spirituality*, 7.

5. Ibid., 7.

6. Ibid., 11.

7. Ibid., 4.

8. Ibid., 8.

9. Şefik Can, *Fundamentals of Rumi's Thought: A Mevlevi Sufi Perspective.* New Jersey: Tughra Books, 2009, 136.

10. Ibid., 137.

11. Ayla Esen Algar, *Architecture, Art and Sufism in Ottoman Turkey* (Berkeley: University of California Press, 1992), 20.

12. Can, *Fundamentals of Rumi's Thought*, 137.

13. Reynold A. Nicholson, *The Mesnevi of Jalalu'ddin Rumi*, Vols. I and II (Lahore: Islamic Book Service, 1989), vol. I, no. 2842.

14. Rumi, *Divan-i Kabir* Vol. III, translated by Bediuzzaman Furuzanfar (Tehran: Darneshgah-e, Tehran, 1957), no. 1414.

15. See Faridun b. Ahmed, *Risale-i Sipehsalar*, trans., Mithat Bahari Beytur (Istanbul: Eles, 2006).

16. Rumi, *The Essential Rumi*, trans. by Coleman Barks and John Moyne (New York: Harper One, 2004), 32.

17. Nasr, *Islamic Art and Spirituality*, 13.

18. Emma Clark, 'The Symbolism of the Islamic Garden,' Islamic Arts & Architecture (October 2, 2011), http://islamic-arts.org/2011/the-symbolism-of-the-islamic-garden/

19. See Qur'an: 20:82, 38:66, 39:5, 40:42, 71:10

20. Can, *Fundamentals of Rumi's Thought*, 271.

21. For more on the philosophy of Yahya Ibn Habash Suhrawardi see Hossein Ziai, *The Book of Radiance* (Tehran: Mazda Publisher, 1998); also see Henry Corbin, *The Man of Light in Iranian Sufism*, trans. Nancy Pearson (New York: Omega Publications, 1994).

22. Can, *Fundamentals of Rumi's Thought*, 273.

23. Celaleddin Rumi, cited in Talat S. Halman, *Rapture and Revolution: Essays on Turkish Literature* (New York: Syracuse University Press, 2007), 297.

24. Henry Corbin, *Alone with the Alone: Creative Imagination in the Sufism of Ibn Arabi*, translated by Ralph Manheim (Princeton, New Jersey: Princeton University Press, 1998), 193.

25. Nasr, *Islamic Art and Spirituality*, 182.

26. Ibid.,107.

27. Suhrawardi, cited in Henry Corbin, *Spiritual Body and Celestial Earth: From Mazdean Iran to Shi'ite Iran*, trans. Nancy Pearson (Princeton, New Jersey: Princeton University Press, 1977), 131.

28. See Corbin, *Alone with the Alone*, 80-81, 145, 182-183.

29. Ibn Arabi, cited in Corbin, *Alone with the Alone*, xvii-xviii.

30. Ibid., xvii-xviii.

31. Ibid., xvii-xviii.

32. Ibid., xvii-xviii.

33. Ibid., 80-81.

34. Nasr, *Islamic Art and Spirituality*, 129, 186.

35. Ibn Arabi, cited in Corbin, *Alone with the Alone*, 80.

36. Ibid., 185, 200-201

37. Corbin, *The Man of Light in Iranian Sufism*, 141.

38. Goethe, cited in Corbin, *The Man of light in Iranian Sufism*, 152.

39. Although there are no explicit Hell imageries depicted in mosques, the many references to 'Hell-Fire' in the supplications adorning the walls of the Rustem Pasha Mosque reflect this view. 'O God! Remove us from the Fire and make us enter Paradise together with the righteous ones by forgiving us with your mercy. For Thou art the most merciful of all.' Translation of the invocation on the window lunette.

40. Nicholson, *The Mesnevi of Jalalu'ddin Rumi*, vol. V, no. 3278.

41. For more see Osman Horata, 'Mevlāna ve Divan Şairleri,' Hacettepe Üniversitesi Edebiyat Fakültesi Dergisi (2008): 47-48, http://akademik.semazen.net/article_detail.php?id=417

42. Carl Brockelmann, *History of Islamic Peoples* (London: Routledge, 1982), 255.

43. Ali Tüfekçi, 'Books, syllabuses, ijazah: A look into the educational system in Ottoman madrassas,' *Daily Sabah* (December 2, 2020), accessed December 11, 2020, https://www.dailysabah.com/arts/books-syllabuses-ijazah-a-look-into-the-educational-system-in-ottoman-madrassas/news; also see Ekmeddin Ihsanoğlu, "The Madrasas of the Ottoman Empire," Foundation for Science Technology and Civilisation (April 2004), accessed December 11, 2020, https://muslimheritage.com/uploads/madrasas.pdf

44. Farrukh Dhondy, *Rumi: A New Translation of Selected Poems* (New York: Arcade Publishing, 2103), 8. Also see Omid Safi, 'Did the Two Oceans Meet? Historical

Connections and Disconnections between Ibn 'Arabi and Rumi,' *Journal of the Muhyiddin Ibn 'Arabi Society* 26 (1999): 55-88, accessed March 5, 2018, https://www.academia.edu/2654506/_Did_the_Two_Oceans_Meet_Historical_-Connections_and_Disconnections_between_Ibn_Arabi_and_Rumi_

45. Fatih Akçe, *The Conqueror of the East: Sultan Selim I* (New Jersey: Blue Dome, 2016), 158.
46. Ibid., 158.
47. Ibid., 158.
48. Ibid., 158.
49. Mehmet Önder, *Mevlāna and the Mevlāna Museum*, edited by Zümrüt Akşit (Istanbul: Akşit Culture and Tourism Publication, 1985), 84.
50. Frembgen, 'Calligraphy from Ottoman Dervish Lodges,' *Islamic Arts and Architecture.*
51. Sufi influence on art, see Önder, *Mevlāna and the Mevlāna Museum*, 66-85. Also see Algar, *Architecture, Art and Sufism in Ottoman Turkey*, 62,
52. Önder, *Mevlāna and the Mevlāna Museum*, 78.
53. Ibid., 68.
54. Ibid., 42.
55. Ibid., 42.
56. For more on the Ottoman Renaissance see Mustafa, *The Ottoman Renaissance.* More specifically see Chapter Six, "Ottoman Fine Arts: Word of God, Art of Man", 131-172.
57. Sa'i, *Sinan's Autobiographies*, 131.
58. Ibid., 132. Kevser in the Qur'an is one the rivers of Paradise.
59. Ibid., 132.
60. Vasari, Preface to Part II, The Lives, http://members.efn.org/~acd/vite/VasariPreface2.html
61. Toby Mayer, 'Theology and Sufism', in *The Cambridge companion to Classical Islamic Theology*, edited by Tim Winter (United Kingdom: Cambridge University Press, 2008), 265.
62. Sa'i, *Sinan's Autobiographies,* 58.
63. Ibid., 64.

3. TECHNOLOGY OF RENAISSANCE ART

1. In Greek mythology, Minos was the king of Crete and was the son of Zeus and Europa. He became one of the three judges of the underworld after his own death and Michelangelo has depicted Minos with ass-ears and wrapped in serpents' coils symbolising the Devil. The coils indicate to what circle of Hell the damned are destined.
2. James A. Connor, *The Last Judgment: Michelangelo and the Death of the Renaissance* (New York: Palgrave and Macmillan, 2009). Kindle Edition.
3. Ibid.
4. Ibid.
5. Ibid.
6. Ibid.
7. Ibid.
8. Ibid.

9. A. Condivi, *The Life of Michelangelo*, trans. Alice Sedgewick Wohl, ed. Helmut Wohl (Baton Rouge: Louisiana State UP, 1976), 83.
10. Vasari, *Lives*, 155.
11. M. Giacometi, ed. *The Sistine Chapel* (New York: Harmony Books, 1986), 190.
12. John O'Malley, "Art, Trent, and Michelangelo's 'Last Judgment'", *Religions* 3 (2012): 355.
13. John T. Paoletti and Gary M. Radke, *Art in Renaissance Italy* (London: Laurence Kink Publishing Ltd, 2005), 505.
14. O'Malley, "Art, Trent, and Michelangelo's 'Last Judgment'", 345.
15. Sam Hammer, "Reading Sixteenth Century Italy through Michelangelo's Last Judgement", accessed February 20, 2015, http://www.arts.cornell.edu/knight_institute/publicationsprizes/discoveries/discoveriesfall1997/06samhammer.pdf, pp.2-4.
16. Walter B. Denny, *The Ceramics of the Mosque of Rustem Pasha and the Environment of Change* (New York: Garland Pub., Thesis Edition, 1977).
17. Michael D. Willis, "Tiles from the Mosque of Rüstem Paşa in Istanbul", *Artibus Asiae*, Vol. 48, No. 3/4, Artibus Asiae Publishers, 1987, 284.
18. Necipoğlu, *The Age of Sinan*, 323-325.
19. Ramazanzade Mehmed, *Tarih-i Nişancı Mehmed Paşa* (Istanbul: Tabhane-yi Amire, 1862), 302-303.
20. Nezihi Aykut, *Hasan-Beyzade Tarihi*, PhD thesis, Istanbul University, 1980, 52.
21. Vakfiye Genel Müdürlüğü (VGM), Defter 648, 176.
22. Denny, *The Ceramics of the Mosque of Rustem Pasha*, 91, 94.
23. Fatih Cimok, *Tiles of Rustem Pasha Mosque* (Istanbul: A Turizm Yayınları, 2001), 11
24. Kuban, *Ottoman Architecture*, 323.
25. Andre Clot, *Suleiman the Magnificent*, trans., Matthew J. Reisz (London: Saqi Books, 2005), 276.
26. Ibid., 86.
27. Gordon Elliot (Producer), *The Genuine Article with Gordon Elliot: IZNIK TILES: Art Renaissance after 300 hundred years*, (15 March, 2012). http://www.youtube.com/watch?v=CU6rvX3UHvY
28. John Covel, cited in J. Raby, "The Making of an Iznik Pot" in *Iznik: The Pottery of Ottoman Turkey*, in N. Atasoy & J. Raby, edited by Y. Petsopoulos (London: Thames & Hudson, 1989), 50.
29. For more on Iznik ware production see Atasoy and Raby, *Iznik: The Pottery of Ottoman Turkey*, 50-64.
30. Ibid., 59.
31. Ibid., 59.
32. Ibid., 58-59.
33. Raby, "The Making of an Iznik Pot" in *Iznik: The Pottery of Ottoman Turkey*, 58.
34. W. D. Kingery and P. B. Vandiver, *Ceramic Masterpieces: Art, Structure and Technology* (New York: Free Press, 1986), 132.
35. Raby, "The Making of an Iznik Pot", 58.

4. MICHELANGELO AND SINAN

1. For more see Qur'an, 53:1-10.
2. See M. Muhsin Khan, trans. *The Translation of the Meanings of Summarized Sahih Al-Bukhari, Arabic-English* (Karachi: Kazi Publications Inc., 1995), 5:58:227.

3. The place of the old Jewish Temple of Solomon and the current Dome of the Rock in Jerusalem. At the time of Muhammad, only the Rock was visible as these structures did not exist – Solomon's Temple had been destroyed by the Romans in 70AD and the Dome of the Rock and Al-Aqsa Mosque had not been built at the same site until 691CE and 705CE respectively.

4. A. Guillaume, *The Life of Muhammad: A translation of Ibn Ishaq's Sirat Rasul Allah* (Oxford: Oxford University Press, 1982), 182.

5. For more on this see Guillaume, *The Life of Muhammad*, 181-187.

6. For more see Abel Pavet de Courteille, *Miradj-Nameh: Recit de l'ascension de Mahomet au ciel, compose ah 840 (1436/1437)* (Paris: Philo Press, 1975). Also see Marie-Rose Seguy, *The Miraculous Journey of Mahomet* (New York: George Braziller, 1977).

7. For the Timurid illustrations from Herat (Afghanistan) see Mir-Heidar's *Mi'raj-name* in Somayeh Ramezanmahi and Hasan Bolkhari Ghehi, "The Manifestation of Fire and Lighting the Icons of Mir-Heidar's Miraj Nameh," *International Journal of Arts*, Vol. 2 No. 4 (2012): 16-25, doi: 10.5923/j.arts.20120204.01.

8. Qur'an, 53:4-18.

9. Süleyman Chelebi, *The Mevlidi Serif*, translated by F. Lyman MacCallum (London: John Murray, 1957), 7, 9.

10. Ibid., 34, 36.

11. For more on Siyer-i Nebi see Fisher, Carol Garrett Fisher, "A Reconstruction of the Pictorial Cycle of the "Siyar-i Nabī" of Murād III", *Ars Orientalis*, Vol. 14, (1984):75–94.

12. See Miguel Asin Palacios, *Islam and the Divine Comedy* (New York: Routledge, 2008), Kindle Edition.

13. See Morris, "The Spiritual Ascension: Ibn 'Arabi and the Mi'raj Pt 1," 638.

14. Ibn Arabi cited in Morris, "The Spiritual Ascension: Ibn 'Arabi and the Mi'raj Pt 1," 632.

15. Carlo Saccone, "Muhammad's Mi 'raj: a legend between East and West," trans. from Italian by Ed Emery, accessed June 14, 2015, https://www.academia.edu/1079798 Muhammads_Miraj_a_legend_between_East_and_West_translated_from_italian_by_Ed_Emery_postface_to_Il_Libro_della_Scala_di_Maometto_SE_Milano_1991_reprint_Mondadori_Milano_1999_IN_Archivi_di_Studi_Indo-Mediterranei_I_2011_

16. See Roger Theodore Lafferty, "The Philosophy of Dante," *Annual Reports of the Dante Society* 30 (1911): 1-34, accessed May 11, 2015, https://www.jstor.org/stable/40165857.

17. Jung, *Man and his Symbols*, 243-44.

18. See Tim Winter, ed., *The Cambridge companion to Classical Islamic Theology* (United Kingdom: Cambridge University Press, 2008); also see De Lacy O'Leary, Islamic Thought and Its Place in History (New Delhi: Goodword Books, 2007).

19. See E. Renan, *Averroes and Averroism* (Paris: Calmann Lévy, 1882); also see Averroes, "Faslul-al Maqal," trans. Hamid Naseem Rafiabadi and Aadil Amin Kak, in *The Attitude of Islam Towards Science and Philosophy* (New Delhi: Sarup & Sons, 2003), 43.

20. Saccone, "Muhammad's Mi 'raj." Palacios, *Islam and the Divine Comedy*. Kindle Edition.

21. Saccone, "Muhammad's Mi 'raj."

22. See Saccone, "Muhammad's Mi 'raj."

23. See Patricia A. Emison, *Creating the "Divine" Artist: From Dante to Michelangelo (Cultures, Beliefs and Traditions Medieval and Early Modern Peoples)* (Leiden: Brill Academic Publication, 2004).

24. Benjamin David, 'The Paradisal Body in Giovanni di Paolo's Illuminations of the "Commedia",' *Dante Studies, with the Annual Report of the Dante Society*, 122, (2004): 45.

25. Dorothy L. Sayers, trans., *The Divine Comedy, Part 3: Paradise* (London: Penguin Classics, 1962), notes on Canto XXX, 323-91.

26. Dante Alighieri, *Paradiso*, trans., Allen Mandelbaum, (New York: A Signet Classic, 1970), Canto XXX, lines 46–54.

27. Sayers, *Paradise*, notes on Canto XXXIII

28. Karen Armstrong, *Muhammad: A Biography of the Prophet* (London: Phoenix, 2001), 139.

29. See Palacios, *Islam and the Divine Comedy*. Kindle Edition.

30. See Palacios, *Islam and the Divine Comedy*.

31. For Ibn Arabi see Henry Corbin, *Alone with the Alone: Creative Imagination in the Sufism of Ibn Arabi*, translated by Ralph Manheim (Princeton: New Jersey: Princeton University Press, 1998).

32. See Saccone, "Muhammad's Mi'raj."

33. Palacios, *Islam and the Divine Comedy*.

34. Ibid.

35. Saccone, "Muhammad's Mi'raj."

36. Michael Camille, *Gothic Art: Glorious Visions* (New York, NY: Harry N. Abrams Inc. Publishing, 1996), 42.

37. Acts 26:12-13 ASV.

38. See Paul Barolsky, "The Visionary Art of Michelangelo in the Light of Dante," *Dante Studies, with the Annual Report of the Dante Society*, 144 (1996): 1-14, accessed May 14, https://www.jstor.org/stable/40166593

39. Ibid., 1.

40. Séguy, *The Miraculous Journey of Mahomet*, 19.

41. Giorgio Vasari, *Lives of the Painters, Sculptors and Architects*, translated by Gaston du C. de Vere with an introduction and Notes by David Ekserdjian (London: Everyman's Library, 1996), 739.

42. For reference to Michelangelo studying all three artists see Anthony Hughes, *Michelangelo* (New York: Phaidon Press Limited, 1997), 38.

43. For reference to Michelangelo focusing most upon the writings of Dante see Washington Gladden, *Witnesses of the Light* (New York: Houghton, Mifflin and Company, 1903.

44. See Gianota Donato, *De'giorni che Dante ʾconsumo nel cercare, l'Inferno e 'l Purgatoria* (Firenze: Nella Tipografia Galileiana, 1859.

45. Leo Lerman, *Michelangelo, a Renaissance Profile* (New York: Knopf, 1948), 52.

46. Sa'i, *Sinan's Autobiographies*, 88.

47. Toby Mayer, 'Theology and Sufism', in *The Cambridge companion to Classical Islamic Theology*, edited by Tim Winter (United Kingdom: Cambridge University Press, 2008), 265.

48. Sa'i, *Sinan's Autobiographies*, 58.

49. Ibid., 64.

50. Guillaume, *The Life of Muhammad*, 181.

5. MICHELANGELO MEETS SINAN

1. For more see John Shearman, *Mannerism* (London: Penguin Books, 1967); also see Ross Finnochio, "Mannerism: Bronzino (1503–1572) and His Contemporaries," in *Heilbrunn Timeline of Art History* (New York: The Metropolitan Museum of Art, New York, 2000 -), accessed July 2, 2015, http://www.metmuseum.org/toah/hd/zino/hd_zino.htm.

2. Marcia B. Hall, 'Michelangelo's Last Judgment: Resurrection of the Body and Predestination,' *The Art Bulletin* 58, No. 1 (March, 1976), 96, College Art Association, accessed May 8, 2014, http://www.jstor.org/stable/3049465; also see Hall Marcia B. Hall, Michelangelo's Last Judgment (New York: Cambridge University Press, 2005).

3. Hall, 'Michelangelo's Last Jugment,' 96.

4. Ibid., 96.

5. Cajetan cited in Hall, 'Michelangelo's Last Judgment,' 96.98.

6. Ibid., 99-100.

7. Ibid., 100.

8. Hall, 'Michelangelo's Last Judgment,' 88.

9. Ibid., 88.

10. Sa'i, *Sinan's Autobiographies*, 64.

11. Ibid., 131.

12. Ibid., 132. Kevser in the Qur'an is one the rivers of Paradise.

13. Ibid., 132. Sixteenth-century Ottoman Renaissance thought and art are influenced by Sufi humanism of Rumi, Ibn Arabi and the classical ideals of Plato. Influence of Rumi on Ottoman literati is immense. Having lived and preached in Seljuk Konya in the thirteenth century, Rumi's work, the *Mesnevi* (*Mathnawi* in English) a spiritual text of 25,000 verses teaching Sufis how to attain their goal of uniting with God and being truly in love with the Divine. This mystical and esoteric understanding of Islam influenced his contemporaries including Yunus Emre (1238-1320). Others followed in the subsequent centuries including Letafi (d.1582), Nef'i (d.1635) and Ismail Rusuhi (d.1630) are among the followers of Rumi. For more on the influence of Rumi on Ottoman consciousness see Osman Horata, 'Mevlāna ve Divan Şairleri,' Hacettepe Üniversitesi Edebiyat Fakültesi Dergisi (2008): 47-48, http://akademik.se-mazen.net/article_detail.php?id=417. On the inlfience of Ibn Arabi on Ottoman thought see Omid Safi, 'Did the Two Oceans Meet? Historical Connections and Disconnections between Ibn 'Arabi and Rumi,' Journal of the Muhyiddin Ibn 'Arabi Society 26 (1999): 55-88, accessed March 5, 2018, https://www.academia.e-du/2654506/_Did_the_Two_Oceans_Meet_Historical_Connections_and_Disconnec-tions_between_Ibn_Arabi_and_Rumi_ Throughout the Seljuk and Ottoman periods, Sufis contributed to the development of Islamic art. The Mevlāna Museum of Konya houses some of the Sufi art works including the earliest manuscript of the *Mesnevi* (1278) and illuminated works from the Seljuk and Ottoman periods. There are numerous Qur'ans inscribed in different calligraphic styles demonstrating the Sufi contributions to the development of this art form throughout the centuries. See Mehmet Önder, *Mevlāna and the Mevlāna Museum*, edited by Zümrüt Akşit (Istanbul: Akşit Culture and Tourism Publication, 1985), 84. Architecturally, reverence for Rumi and his Sufi order by the Ottoman sultans in the sixteenth century can be seen through the restoration of the master's tomb. As Mehmet Önder states: "During the reign of Süleyman the Magnificent, Sinan, the leading architect of the day built a *semahane* [assembly hall for whirling ceremonies] and a *mescid* [chapel] in the

complex on imperial orders. The domed dervish cells were surrounding the mausoleum were built during the reign of Murad III [d.1595], on his orders, and the monumental fountain – şadırvan – in the courtyard was built during the period of Selim the Grim [d.1520]." Önder, *Mevlāna and the Mevlāna Museum*, 68.

14. For more see Shearman, *Mannerism*; also see C. de Tolnay, *Michelangelo: Sculptor, Painter, Architect* (New York: Princeton University, Press,1975), 50.

15. A. Leader, 'Michelangelo's Last Judgment: The Culmination of Papal Propaganda in the Sistine Chapel,' *Studies in Iconography*, 27 (2006): 106, accessed March 12, 2014, https://www.academia.edu/467863/Michelangelos_Last_Judgment_The_Culmination_of_Papal_Propaganda_in_the_Sistine_Chapel

16. For more see Cornell Fleischer, "The Lawgiver as Messiah: The Making of the Imperial Image in the Reign of Suleyman," in *Soliman le magnifique et son temps*, edited by Gilles Veinstein (Paris: La Documentation Française, 1992).

17. Hall, 'Michelangelo's Last Judgment,' 89.

18. Ibid., 89.

19. Paul Klee cited in Jung, *Man and his Symbols*, 267.

20. L. Steinberg, 'Michelangelo's Last Judgement as Merciful Heresy,' Art in America 63 (1975), 63, accessed August 11, 2016, https://www.artinamericamagazine.com/news-features/magazines/from-the-archives-michelangelos-last-judgement-as-merciful-heresy/

21. Hammer, "Reading Sixteenth-Century Italy through Michelangelo's Last Judgement."

22. C. de Tolnay, *Michelangelo: The Final Period* (New York: Princeton University Press, 1960), 30.

23. Hall, 'Michelangelo's Last Judgment,' 85.

24. New Testament, Paul 1, Corinthians 15.

25. For more on flower symbolism of Iznik tiles in the Rustem Pasha Mosque see Mustafa, *The Ottoman Renaissance*, 131-172.

26. Ramazanzade Mehmed, *Tarih-i Nişancı Mehmed Paşa*, 302-3.

27. For more on the tulip and its symbolic association with Allah see Mike Dash, *Tulipomania: The Story of the World's Most Coveted Flower and the Extraordinary Passions it Aroused* (London: Phoenix, 2011).

28. Qur'an: 57:4.

29. Ogier Ghiselinde Busbecq, *The Turkish Letters of Ogier Ghiselin de Busbecq*, trans. Edward Seymour Forster (Oxford: Clarendon Press, 1968), 28.

30. See Talat S. Halman, ed., *Yunus Emre and His Mystical Poetry* (Indianapolis: Indiana University Press, 1983).

31. For the mystical meaning of the tulip see I. Melikoff, "La fleur de la souffrance. Recherche sur le sens symbolique de Lâle dans ka poésie mystique turco-iranienne,'" *Journal Asiatique* 205 (1967): 341-60. For more on Süleyman's poetry see Talat S. Halman, *Süleyman the Magnificent Poet* (Istanbul: Reyo Ofset, 1987).

32. Paul Smith, *Turkish Sufi Poets: Lives and Poems* (Victoria, Australia: New Humanity Books, 2014), 32.

33. J. M. Rogers and R. M. Ward, *Süleyman the Magnificent* (London: British Museum Publications, 1990), 85-89.

34. Qur'an: 59:24.

35. Qur'an: 13:24-25.

36. Cimok, *Tiles of Rustem Pasha Mosque*, 12.

37. Ibn Arabi cited in, Corbin, *Alone with the Alone*, 145.

38. Folio 281a clearly depicts the simurg in the *Surname-i Hümayun* illustrated manuscript of 1582 flying over the procession of the guilds before Murad III.

39. Zulfi Güler, "Symbols of Anka and Simurg in Sheikh Galib's Diwan", *International Journal of Language Academy* 2 (2014): 63, accessed June 3, 2015, http://www.i-jla.net/Makaleler/2069338573_6372%20Zülfi%20Güler%20(1)%20(2).pdf. It is also used in expression of some elements as "beauty, dignity, modesty, disinterestedness, knowledge, talent, enlightenment, illumination and regeneration via metaphors and analogies", 63.

40. Özlem Inay Erten and Oğuz Erten, *Turkish Tiles*, translated by Niki Gamm (Istanbul: Silk Road Publications, 2013), 34.

41. Denny, *Iznik: The Artistry of Ottoman Ceramics*, 91.

42. Qur'an, 56:10-38.

43. Reynold A. Nicholson, *The Mesnevi of Jalalu'ddin Rumi*, Vols. I and II (Lahore: Islamic Book Service, 1989), vol. I, no.316.

44. Ibid., no.311, 1353.

45. Celaleddin Rumi, cited in Talat S. Halman, *Rapture and Revolution: Essays on Turkish Literature* (New York: Syracuse University Press, 2007), 297.

46. Skirt, as a piece of cloth can be laid flat on a surface imitating prostration and submission. Süleyman, as the slave of God, resembles himself to a piece of cloth like a skirt who humbles himself before Him.

47. Talat S. Halman, *Süleyman the Magnificent Poet* (Istanbul: Reyo Ofset, 1987), 37.

48. Sarah Melanie Rolfe, 'Michelangelo Reading Landino? The 'Devil' in Michelangelo's Last Judgement,' *Quaderni d'italianistica*, Volume XXX, No. 2 (2009): 24.

49. Dante Alighieri, "Inferno: Canto V," in *Divine Comedy of Dante Alighieri*, translated by Henry Wadsworth Longfellow (Pennsylvania: Pennsylvania State University, 2005), 21, accessed October 13, 2015, http://swcta.net/moore/files/2013/10/dante-longfellow.pdf.

50. Steinberg, 'The Last Judgment as Merciful Heresy,' 53.

51. Loren W. Partridge, *Michelangelo, The Last Judgment: A Glorious Restoration*, with texts by F. Mancinelli and G. Collalucci (New York: Abradale Press 1997), 8.

52. Dante, "Inferno: Canto V," 16, 55, 136.

53. Rolfe, 'Michelangelo Reading Landino?', 28.

54. Rolfe, 'Michelangelo Reading Landino?', 28.

55. James M. Saslow, *The Poetry of Michelangelo: An Annotated Translation* (New York: Yale University Press, 1991), 208.

56. Ibid., 135-136.

57. For more on the Jungian shadow ("fed by the neglected and repressed collective values") see Connie Zweig and Jeremiah Abrams, eds., *Meeting the Shadow: The Hidden Power of the Dark Side of Human Nature* (New York: Penguin Putnam Inc., 1991), 4-5; also see Jung, *Man and his Symbols*, 82.

58. Translations of the invocations of the window lunettes from Rustem Pasha Mosque.

59. Translations of the invocations of the window lunettes from Rustem Pasha Mosque.

60. Qur'an, 24:35.

61. For more see Nuha N. N. Khoury, "The Mihrab: From Text to Form," *International Journal of Middle East Studies* Vol. 30, No. 1 (1998): 1-27, accessed December 14, 2020, https://www.jstor.org/stable/164202?readnow=1&refreqid=excel-sior%3A1166c8f907fd5a2d2ec74f2be9a328&seq=1

62. Sa'i, *Sinan's Autobiographies*, 132.

63. See Wassily Kandinsky, *Concerning the Spiritual in Art*, trans., M. T. H. Sadler (New York: Dover Publications, Inc., 1977). 157, 181-82.

64. Kandinsky, *Concerning the Spiritual in Art*, 157-58.

65. Cimok, *Book of Rustem Pasha Tiles*, 21.

66. See M. M. Khan, trans., *The Translation of the Meanings of Summarized Sahih Al-Bukhari* (Lahore: Kazi Publications Inc., 1995).

67. Cimok, *Book of Rustem Pasha Tiles*, 21; also see the Qur'an, 51:62-65.

68. See Lisa Golombek, "The Draped Universe of Islam", accessed June 25, 2015, https://s3.amazonaws.com/files.digication.com/M05f7bff842e90d2d36e67917c-dac3d50

69. For more see Oleg Grabar, The Dome of the Rock (Cambridge, MA: Harvard University Press, 2006), 189-204. In particular, see pp.196-199 regarding the Qur'anic verses chosen to represent this view.

70. Qur'an: 13:11, 21:47, 59:18, and 91:9.

71. William E. Wallace, *Michelangelo: The Artist, the Man, and His Times* (New York: Cambridge University Press, 2010), Kindle Edition.

72. Jalaluddin Rumi, *Divan-i Kabir*, translated by Bediuzzaman Furuzanfar (Tehran: Darneshgah-e, 1957), Vol. I, no. 338.

73. Nicholson, *Mesnevi*, vol. I, no. 733.

74. Richard Etlin, 'Aesthetic and the Spatial Sense of Self,' *Journal of Aesthetics and Art Criticism*, Vol. 56/1, (Winter 1998):1.

75. Patricia Trutty-Coohill, "Agathos in Michelangelo's Sistine Ceiling", accessed June 28, 2015, http://www.agathos-international-review.com/issue1/articles/01_A-GATHOS_IN_MICHELANGELO_SISTINE_CEILING.pdf, 12.

76. Nicholson, *Mesnevi*, vol. 1, no. 1341.

77. Ibid., vol. 1, no. 1341.

78. Franz Marc cited in Jung, *Man and his Symbols*, 262.

79. The New Testament, Matthew 25: "And the wicked shall say to him, 'Lord, when did we see you hungry or thirsty or naked or sick or imprisoned or away from home?' and the King will say to them 'As long as you refused to do this to one of my least brothers and sisters, you refused to do it to me.'"

80. Connor, *The Last Judgment*.

81. C. de Tolnay, *Michelangelo: The Final Period*, 30.

82. Giacometi, *The Sistine Chapel*, 178.

83. Connor, *The Last Judgment*.

84. Ibid.

85. Ibid.

86. Hall, 'Michelangelo's Last Judgment,' 89.

87. A. Condivi cited in Hall, 'Michelangelo's Last Judgment,' 91.

88. Denny, *Iznik: The Artistry of Ottoman Ceramics*, 86.

89. Ibid., 86.

90. The New Testament, Matthew 25: 33

91. Hall, 'Michelangelo's Last Judgment,' 89, 91.

92. Ibid., 91.

93. Ibid., 91.

94. Qur'an, 4:70, 10:99, 54:49.

95. Can, *Fundamentals of Rumi's Thought*, 223.

96. Ibid., 223.

CONCLUSION

1. Jung, *Man and his Symbols*, 89.
2. Jung, *Man and his Symbols*, 18.
3. V. Kandinsky, 'Reflexions sur l'art abstrait', *Cahiers d'Art*, 6 (1931): 350-351.

BIBLIOGRAPHY

Adler, F. 'Die Moscheen zu Constantinopel: Eine architektonische baugeschictliche Studie,' (The Mosques of Constantinople: An Architectural Study). *Deutsche Bauzeitung* 8 (1874).

Ahmed, F. *Risale-i Sipehsalar*. Translated by Mithat Bahari Beytur. Istanbul: Eles, 2006.

Akçe, F. *The Conqueror of the East: Sultan Selim I*. New Jersey: Blue Dome, 2016.

Algar, Ayla E. *Architecture, Art and Sufism in Ottoman Turkey*. Berkeley: University of California Press, 1992.

Alighieri, D. *Divine Comedy of Dante Alighieri*. Translated by Henry Wadsworth Longfellow. Pennsylvania: Pennsylvania State University, 2005. Accessed October 13, 2015. http://swc-ta.net/moore/files/2013/10/dante-longfellow.pdf.

Alighieri, D. *Paradiso*. Translated by Allen Mandelbaum. New York: A Signet Classic, 1970.

Aristotle. "Nicomachean Ethics," Book IV. Accessed March 22, 2015. http://www.sacred-texts.com/cla/ari/nico/nico036.htm

Armstrong, Karen. *Muhammad: A Biography of the Prophet.* London: Phoenix, 2001.

Atasoy, N. and Julian Raby. *Iznik: The Pottery of Ottoman Turkey.* Edited by Yanni Petsopoulos. London: Thames and Hudson, 1989.

Atıl, E. *Süleymanname: The Illustrated History of Süleyman the Magnificent.* Washington: National Gallery of Art, 1986.

Atıl, E. 'The Image of Süleyman in Ottoman Art.' In *Süleyman the Second and His Time.* Edited by Halil Inalcik and Cemal Kafadar, 333-341. Istanbul: The Isis Press, 2010.

Averroes. "Faslul-al Maqal." In *The Attitude of Islam Towards Science and Philosophy,* translated by Hamid Naseem Rafiabadi and Aadil Amin Kak. New Delhi: Sarup & Sons, 2003.

Aykut, N. *Hasan-Beyzade Tarihi.* PhD thesis, Istanbul University, 1980.

Babinger, F. 'Die türkische Renaissance: Bemerkungen zum Schaffen des grossen türkischen Baumeisters Sinân.' *Beiträge zur Kenntnis des Orients* 9 (1914): 67–88.

Babinger, F. 'Ein osmanischer Michelangelo.' *Frankfurter Zeitung,* Sept. 7, 1915, no. 248.

Barolsky, Paul. "The Visionary Art of Michelangelo in the Light of Dante." *Dante Studies, with the Annual Report of the Dante Society,* 144 (1996): 1-14. Accessed May 14, 2015. https://www.jstor.org/stable/40166593

Baron, H. *The Crisis of the Early Italian Renaissance.* Princeton: Princeton University Press, 1966.

Besnier- Kılıçioğlu, S. 'Sinan and Palladio: The Parallel Development of Two Master-Builders.' *The UNESCO Courier: a window open on the world* XLI, no. 3 (1988). Accessed March 4, 2014. http://unesdoc.un-esco.org/images/0007/000781/078126eo.pdf#77905

Bhabha, H. *The Location of Cultures.* London & New York: Routledge, 1994. Kindle Edition.

Bisaha, N. *Creating East and West: Renaissance Humanists and the Ottoman Turks.* Philadelphia: University of Pennsylvania Press, 2006.

Brewster, D. P. 'The Study of Sufism: Towards a methodology.' Accessed June 24, 2017. https://www.sciencedirect.com/sdfe/pdf/download/eid/1-s2.0-0048721X76900476/first-page-pdf, 31.

Brockelmann, C. *History of Islamic Peoples.* London: Routledge, 1982.

Brotton, J. *The Renaissance: A Very Short Introduction.* New York: Oxford University Press, 2006.

Brotton, J. *The Renaissance Bazaar: From the Silk Road to Michelangelo.* New York: Oxford University Press, 2002. Kindle Edition.

Burckhardt, J. *The Civilisation of the Renaissance in Italy.* Pisa: Aonia edizioni, 2011.

Burioni, M. 'Vasari's Rinascita: History, Anthropology or Art Criticism.' Accessed January 29, 2016. https://www.academia.edu/2638258/Vasari_s_rinascita._History_anthropology_or_art_criticis

Burns, Howard. "Building and Construction in Palladio's Vicenza." In *Les Chantiers de la renaissance.* Edited by A. Chastel and J. Guillaume, 191-226. Paris: Picard, 1991.

Busbecq, O. G. *The Turkish Letters of Ogier Ghiselin de Busbecq.* Translated by Edward Seymour Forster Oxford: Clarendon Press, 1968.

Camille, Michael. *Gothic Art: Glorious Visions.* New York, NY: Harry N. Abrams Inc. Publishing, 1996.

Can, Şefik. *Fundamentals of Rumi's Thought: A Mevlevi Sufi Perspective.* New Jersey: Tughra Books, 2009.

Castellano, D. J. 'The Renaissance Concept of Self as seen in Petrarch, Castiglione and Montaigne.' Massachusetts: Boston University, 2002. Accessed May 23, 2016. http://www.arcaneknowledge.org/histschol/renaissance.htm

Chelebi, Süleyman. *The Mevlidi Serif*. Translated by F. Lyman MacCallum. London: John Murray, 1957.

Cimok, Fatih. *Tiles of Rustem Pasha Mosque*. Istanbul: A Turizm Yayınları, 2001.

Clark, E. 'The Symbolism of the Islamic Garden.' Islamic Arts & Architecture (October 2, 2011). Accessed March 23, 2016. http://islamic-arts.org/2011/the-symbolism-of-the-islamic-garden/

Clot, A. *Suleiman the Magnificent*. Translated by Matthew J. Reisz. London: Saqi Books, 2005.

Coles, P. *Ottoman Impact on Europe*. Harcourt: Brace & World, 1968.

Condivi, Ascanio. *The Life of Michelangelo*. Translated by Alice Sedgwick Wohl. Oxford: Phaidon Press Limited, 1976.

Connor, J. A. *The Last Judgment: Michelangelo and the Death of the Renaissance*. New York: Palgrave and Macmillan, 2009. Kindle Edition.

Connors, Joseph. 'Borromini, Hagia Sophia, and S. Vitale.' *Architectural Studies in Memory of Richard Krautheimer*. ed. Cecil Striker. Mainz: Verlag Philipp Von Zabern, 1996: 43-48.

'Contemplation, Constructed Space, and Senses.' YouTube Video. Lecture by Phoebe Crisman with an introduction by Kim Tanzer, April 6, 2013, posted by University of Virginia Contemplative Sciences Center, August 19, 2013. Accessed May 5, 2015. http://www.youtube.com/watch?v=6FASJrighYE

Corbin, Henry. *Alone with the Alone: Creative Imagination in the Sufism of Ibn Arabi*. Translated by Ralph Manheim. Princeton, New Jersey: Princeton University Press, 1998.

Corbin, H. *Spiritual Body and Celestial Earth: From Mazdean Iran to Shi'ite Iran*. Translated by Nancy Pearson. Princeton, New Jersey: Princeton University Press, 1977.

Corbin, H. *The Man of Light in Iranian Sufism*. Translated by Nancy Pearson. New York: Omega Publications, 1994.

Courteille, Abel Pavet de. *Miradj-Nameh: Recit de l'ascension de Mahomet au ciel, compose ah 840 (1436/1437).* Paris: Philo Press, 1975.

Dash, M. *Tulipomania: The Story of the World's Most Coveted Flower and the Extraordinary Passions it Aroused.* London: Phoenix, 2011.

David, Benjamin. 'The Paradisal Body in Giovanni di Paolo's Illuminations of the "Commedia." *Dante Studies, with the Annual Report of the Dante Society* 122, (2004): 45-69.

Denny, Walter B. *Iznik: The Artistry of Ottoman Ceramics.* London, UK: Thames and Hudson, 2010.

Denny, W. B. *The Ceramics of the Mosque of Rustem Pasha and the Environment of Change.* New York: Garland Pub., Thesis Edition, 1977.

Dhondy, F. *Rumi: A New Translation of Selected Poems.* New York: Arcade Publishing, 2013.

Diez, E. *Türk Sanatı: Başlangıcından Günümüze Kadar.* Translated by Oktay Aslanapa. Istanbul, 1946.

Donato, Gianota. *De'giorni che Dante consumo nel cercare, l'Inferno e 'l Purgatoria.* Firenze: Nella Tipografia Galileiana, 1859.

Elliot, G. (Producer). *The Genuine Article with Gordon Elliot: IZNIK TILES: Art Renaissance after 300 hundred years,* (15 March, 2012). http://www.youtube.com/watch?v=CU6rvX3UHvY

Emison, Patricia A. *Creating the "Divine" Artist: From Dante to Michelangelo (Cultures, Beliefs and Traditions Medieval and Early Modern Peoples).* Leiden: Brill Academic Publication, 2004.

Erten, Özlem Inay and Oğuz Erten. *Turkish Tiles.* Translated by Niki Gamm. Istanbul: Silk Road Publications, 2013.

Etlin, Richard. 'Aesthetic and the Spatial Sense of Self.' *Journal of Aesthetics and Art Criticism,* Vol. 56/1, (Winter 1998): 1-19.

Finnochio, Ross. "Mannerism: Bronzino (1503–1572) and His Contemporaries." In *Heilbrunn Timeline of Art History*. New York: The Metropolitan Museum of Art, New York, 2000 -. Accessed July 2, 2015. http://www.metmuseum.org/toah/hd/zino/hd_zino.htm.=

Fisher, Carol Garrett. "A Reconstruction of the Pictorial Cycle of the "Siyar-i Nabī" of Murād III." *Ars Orientalis*, Vol. 14, (1984):75–94.

Ferguson, W. K. *The Renaissance in Historical Thought*. Cambridge, MA: Houghton Mifflin Company, 1948.

Fleischer, Cornell. "The Lawgiver as Messiah: The Making of the Imperial Image in the Reign of Suleyman." In *Soliman le magnifique et son temps*, edited by Gilles Veinstein. Paris: La Documentation Française, 1992.

Frembgen, J. W. 'Calligraphy from Ottoman Dervish Lodges.' Islamic Arts and Architecture (September 5, 2013). http://islamic-arts.org/2013/calligraphy-from-ottoman-dervish-lodges/.

Giacometi, M. ed., *The Sistine Chapel*. New York: Harmony Books, 1986.

Gladden, Washington. *Witnesses of the Light*. New York: Houghton, Mifflin and Company, 1903. 1-285.

Golombek, Lisa. 'The Draped Universe of Islam.' Accessed June 25, 2015. https://s3.amazonaws.com/files.digication.com/M05f7bf-f842e90d2d36e67917cdac3d50

Gombrich, E. H. *Norm and Form: Studies in the Art of the Renaissance*. London: Phaidon Press, 1966.

Goodwin, Godfrey. *A History of Ottoman Architecture*. London: Thames & Hudson, 1971.

Grabar, Oleg. *The Dome of the Rock*. Cambridge, MA: Harvard University Press, 2006.

Guillaume, A. *The Life of Muhammad: A translation of Ibn Ishaq's Sirat Rasul Allah*. Oxford: Oxford University Press, 1982.

Gurlitt, C. *Istanbul'un Mimari Sanatı, Architecture of Constantinople, Die Baukunst Konstantinopels*. Translated by Rezan Kæzæltan. Ankara: Enformasyon ve Dokumantasyon Hizmetleri Vakfı, 1999.

Güler, Zulfi. 'Symbols of Anka and Simurg in Sheikh Galib's Diwan.' *International Journal of Language Academy* 2 (2014): 63-72. Accessed June 3, 2015. http://www.ijla.net/Makaleler/2069338573_6372%20Zül-fi%20Güler%20(1)%20(2).pdf.

Hall, Marcia B. 'Michelangelo's Last Judgment: Resurrection of the Body and Predestination.' *The Art Bulletin* 58, No. 1 (March, 1976): 85-92. College Art Association. Accessed May 8, 2014. http://www.js-tor.org/stable/3049465

Hall Marcia B. *Michelangelo's Last Judgment*. New York: Cambridge University Press, 2005.

Halman, Talat S. *Rapture and Revolution: Essays on Turkish Literature*. New York: Syracuse University Press, 2007.

Halman, Talat S. *Süleyman the Magnificent Poet*. Istanbul: Reyo Ofset, 1987.

Halman, T. S. *Yunus Emre and His Mystical Poetry*. Indianapolis: Indiana University Press, 1983.

Hammer, Sam. 'Reading Sixteenth-Century Italy through Michelange-lo's Last Judgement. Accessed February 22, 2016. http://www.arts.cor-nell.edu/knight_institute/publicationsprizes/discoveries/discoveriesfall1997/

Hankins, J. 'Renaissance Crusaders: Humanist Crusade Literature in the Age of Mehmed II.' In *Dumbarton Oaks Papers*, Vol. 49. Symposium on Byzantium and the Italians, 13th-15th Centuries (1995): 111-207.

Hartt, F. *History of Italian Renaissance Art* (6th ed.) Englewood Cliffs: Prentice Hall, 2006.

Hentsch, T. *Imagining the Middle East*. Montreal: Black Rose Books, 1992.

Hill, S. 'The Spectacle of the 'Other''. In *Representation: Cultural Representations and Signifying Practices*. Edited by Stuart Hill. London: Sage Publications, 2003.

Horata, O. 'Mevlāna ve Divan Şairleri.' *Hacettepe Üniversitesi Edebiyat Fakültesi Dergisi* (2008): 47-48. Accessed April 24, 2016. http://akademik.semazen.net/article_detail.php?id=417

Hughes, Anthony. *Michelangelo*. New York: Phaidon Press Limited, 1997.

Hughes, Arthur. 'Interpreting the Renaissance.' *Oxford Art Journal* 11 (1988): 77-78.

Ihsanoğlu, E. "The Madrasas of the Ottoman Empire." Foundation for Science Technology and Civilisation (April 2004). Accessed December 11, 2020. https://muslimheritage.com/uploads/madrasas.pdf

Inalcık, H. *The Ottoman Empire: The Classical Age 1300–1600*. London: Butler & Tanner, 1973.

'Interview with Gülru Necipoğlu,' by Gizem Tongo. Department of History at Bogaziçi University, Istanbul, August 2009. Accessed August 15, 2017. http://isites.harvard.edu/fs/docs/icb.topic732589.files//Gizem_Tongo_Interview-GULRU_NECIPOGLU.pdf

Jardine, L. *Worldly Goods: A New History of the Renaissance*. New York: W. W. Norton & Company, Inc., 1996.

Jung, C. G. *Man and his Symbols*. New York: Anchor Press, 1964.

Kandinsky, W. *Concerning the Spiritual in Art*. Translated by M. T. H. Sadler. New York: Dover Publications, Inc., 1977.

Kandinsky, V. 'Reflexions sur l'art abstrait'. *Cahiers d'Art*, 6 (1931): 350-351.

Khan, M. Muhsin, trans. *The Translation of the Meanings of Summarized Sahih Al-Bukhari, Arabic-English*. Lahore: Kazi Publications Inc., 1995.

Khoury, N. N. N. "The Mihrab: From Text to Form," *International Journal of Middle East Studies* Vol. 30, No. 1 (1998): 1-27, accessed December 14, 2020, https://www.jstor.org/stable/164202?read-now=1&refreqid=excelsior%3A3a1166c8f907fd5a2d2ec74f2be9a328&seq1

Kingery, W. D. and P. B. Vandiver. *Ceramic Masterpieces: Art, Structure and Technology*. New York: Free Press, 1986.

Kostof, Spiro. *A History of Architecture: Settings and Rituals* (2nd ed.). Oxford: Oxford University Press, 1995.

Kuban, Doğan. *Ottoman Architecture*. Suffolk: Antique Collectors Club Distributors, 2010.

Lafferty, Roger Theodore. "The Philosophy of Dante." *Annual Reports of the Dante Society* 30 (1911): 1-34. Accessed May 11, 2015. https://www.jstor.org/stable/40165857.

Leader, A. "Michelangelo's Last Judgment: The Culmination of Papal Propaganda in the Sistine Chapel.' *Studies in Iconography* 27 (2006): 103-156. Accessed March 12, 2014. https://www.academia.edu/467863/Michelangelos_Last_Judgment_The_Culmination_of_Papal_Propaganda_in_the_Sistine_Chapel

Lehning, J. R. *To be a Citizen: The Political Culture of the Early French Third Republic*. London: Cornell University Press, 2001.

Lerman, Leo. *Michelangelo, a Renaissance Profile*. New York: Knopf, 1948.

Lewis, B. *Islam and the West*. London: Oxford University Press, 1993.

Libbrecht, U. "Comparative Philosophy: A Methodological Approach." In *Worldviews and Cultures: Philosophical Reflections from an Intercultural Perspective*. Edited by Nicole Note et al. Brussels: Springer, 2009.

Lowenthal, D. *The Past is a Foreign Country*. Cambridge: Cambridge University Press, 1985.

MacClean, G. 'Introduction: Re-Orienting the Renaissance.' In *Re-Orienting the Renaissance: Cultural Exchanges With the East*. Edited by Gerald MacClean. New York: Palgrave Macmillan, 2005.

Mack, R. E. *Bazaar to Piazza: Islamic Trade and Italian Art, 1300-1600.* Berkeley: University of California, 2002.

Madison, Soyini D. *Critical Ethnography: Method, Ethics, and Performance.* Los Angeles: Sage Publications, 2012.

Manetti, Antonio di Tuccio. *The Life of Brunelleschi.* Translated by Catherine Engass. Pennsylvania: Pennsylvania State University Press, 1970.

Matthews, H. 'Rethinking Ottoman Architecture.' Paper presented at the ACSA International Conference, 2001.

Mayer, T. 'Theology and Sufism.' In *The Cambridge companion to Classical Islamic Theology,* edited by Tim Winter, 258-307. United Kingdom: Cambridge University Press, 2008.

McLaughlin, M. L. 'Humanist Concept of Renaissance and Middle Ages in the Tre-and Quattrocento.' *Renaissance Studies* 2 (1988): 131-42.

Melikoff, I. "La fleur de la souffrance. Recherche sur le sens symbolique de Lâle dans ka poésie mystique turco-iranienne.'" *Journal Asiatique* 205 (1967): 341-60.

Michelangelo. *The Complete Poems of Michelangelo.* Translated by John Frederick Nims Chicago: University of Chicago Press, 2000.

Milton, Henry A., and Craig Hugh Smyth. *Michelangelo Architect: The Façade of San Lorenzo and the Drum of the Dome of St. Peter's.* Milan: Olivetti, 1988.

Milton, Henry A., and V. Lampugnani, eds. *The Renaissance from Brunelleschi to Michelangelo: The Representation of Architecture.* Milan: Rizzoli, 1994.

Morkoc, Selen B. "An Architect to Challenge Them All: Sinan Phenomenon in Architectural Historiography." *Fabrications: The Journal of the Society of Architectural Historians, Australia and New Zealand* 19, no. 1 (June 2009): 6-25.

Morkoç, Selen B. "Reading Architecture from the Text: The Ottoman Story of the Four Marble Columns." Accessed February 9, 2018. https://www.academia.edu/27608699/Reading_Architecture_from_-Text_The_Story_of_the_Four_Marble_Columns, 34.

Murray, P. and L. Murray. *The Art of the Renaissance*. London: Thames and London, 1963.

Mustafa, M. *The Ottoman Renaissance: A Reconsideration of Early Modern Ottoman Art, 1413-1575*. New Jersey: Blue Dome Press, 2019.

Nagel, A. and Christopher Wood. "Towards a New Model of Renaissance Anachronism." *Art Bulletin 87* (2005): 403-32.

Nasr, S. H. *Islamic Art and Spirituality*. New York: State University of New York Press, 1987.

New Testament.

Necipoğlu, Gülru. *The Age of Sinan: Architectural Culture in the Ottoman Empire*. London: Reaktion Books, 2005.

Necipoğlu, Gülru. 'Challenging the Past: Sinan and the Competitive Discourse of Early Modern Islamic Architecture.' *Muqarnas* vol. 10. Leiden: Brill, 1993: 169–180. http://www.jstor.org/stable/1523183?seq=1#page_scan_tab_contents

Necipoğlu, Gülru. 'Creation of a National Genius: Sinan and the Historiography of 'Classical' Ottoman Architecture.' *Muqarnas* vol. 24. Leiden: Brill, 2006. http://isites.harvard.edu/fs/docs/icb.topic570061.files//articles/Creation_Genius.pdf

Necipoğlu-Kafadar, G. "The Süleymaniye Complex in Istanbul: An Interpretation." *Muqarnas 3* (1985): 92-117. Accessed February 19, 2015. 2018http://www.jstor.org/stable/1523086?origin=JSTOR-pdf, 92.

Nicholson, Reynold A. *The Mesnevi of Jalalu'ddin Rumi*, Vols. I and II. Lahore: Islamic Book Service, 1989.

Norton, C. 'Blurring the Boundaries: Intellectual and Cultural Interactions between Eastern and Western: Christian and Muslim World.' In *The Renaissance and the Ottoman World*. Edited by Anna Contadini and Claire Norton. England: Ashgate Publishing Limited, 2013.

O'Leary, De Lacy. *Islamic Thought and Its Place in History*. New Delhi: Goodword Books, 2007.

O'Malley, J. "Art, Trent, and Michelangelo's 'Last Judgment'". *Religions* 3 (2012): 344-56.

Önder, Mehmet. *Mevlāna and the Mevlāna Museum*. Edited by Zümrüt Akşit Istanbul: Akşit Culture and Tourism Publication, 1985.

Palacios, Miguel Asin. *Islam and the Divine Comedy*. New York: Routledge, 2008. Kindle Edition.

Panofsky, E. *Renaissance and Renascences in Western Art*. Stockholm: Almqvist & Wiksell, 1969.

John T. Paoletti and Gary M. Radke. *Art in Renaissance Italy*. London: Laurence Kink Publishing Ltd, 2005.

Partridge, Loren W. *Michelangelo, The Last Judgment: A Glorious Restoration*, with texts by F. Mancinelli and G. Collalucci. New York: Abradale Press 1997.

Qur'an.

Raby, J. "The Making of an Iznik Pot." In *Iznik: The Pottery of Ottoman Turkey*. N.

Atasoy & J. Raby. Edited by Y. Petsopoulos, 50-64. London: Thames & Hudson, 1989.

Ramachandran, Ayesha. *The Worldmakers: Global Imagining in Early Modern Europe*. Chicago: The University of Chicago Press, 2015.

Ramazanzade, M. *Tarih-i Nişancı Mehmed Paşa*. Istanbul: Tabhane-yi Amire, 1862.

Ramezanmahi, Somayeh, and Hasan Bolkhari Ghehi. "The Manifestation of Fire and Lighting the Icons of Mir-Heidar's Miraj Nameh." *International Journal of Arts*, Vol. 2 No. 4 (2012): 16-25. doi: 10.5923/j.arts.20120204.01.

Raymond, George L. *Art in Theory: An Introduction to the study of comparative aesthetics.* New York: G. T. Putnam Sons, 1894.

Renan, E. *Averroes and Averroism.* Paris: Calmann Lévy, 1882.

Rolfe, Sarah Melanie. 'Michelangelo Reading Landino? The 'Devil'. In Rogers, J. M. and R. M. Ward, *Süleyman the Magnificent.* London: British Museum Publications, 1990.

Ruggiero, Guido, ed. *A Companion to the Worlds of the Renaissance.* Malden: MA: Blackwell Publishing, 2007.

Rumi. *Divan-i Kabir* Vol. III. Translated by Bediuzzaman Furuzanfar. Tehran: Darneshgah-e, Tehran, 1957.

Rumi, Jalaluddin. *Divan-i Kabir.* Translated by Bediuzzaman Furuzanfar. Tehran: Darneshgah-e, 1957.

Rüsen, Jörn. "What is Historical Consciousness? - A Theoretical Approach to Empirical Evidence." Translated by Wolfgang Gebhard. Paper presented at Canadian Historical Consciousness in an International Context: Theoretical Frameworks, University of British Columbia, Vancouver, BC, 2001.

Rolfe, S. M. "Michelangelo's 'Last Judgement.'" *Quaderni d'italianistica*, Volume XXX, No. 2 (2009):19-38.

Saccone, Carlo. "Muhammad's *Mi 'raj*: a legend between East and West." Translated from Italian by Ed Emery. Accessed June 14, 2015. https://www.academia.edu/1079798/

Safi, Omid. 'Did the Two Oceans Meet? Historical Connections and Disconnections between Ibn 'Arabi and Rumi.' *Journal of the Muhyiddin Ibn 'Arabi Society* 26 (1999): 55-88. Accessed March 5, 2018. https://www.academia.edu/2654506/_Did_the_Two_Oceans_Meet_Historical_Connections_and_Disconnections_between_Ibn_Arabi_and_Rumi_

Sa'i, Mustafa. *Sinan's Autobiographies: Five Sixteenth Century Texts*. Introductory Notes, Critical Editions, and Translations by Howard Crane and Esra Akin, edited by Gülru Necipoğlu. Leiden: Brill, 2006.

Said, E. *Orientalism*. London: Penguin Books, 1995.

Sanstead, L. "The Meaning of Michelangelo's David" (5 September 2004). Accessed February 19, 2017. http://www.sandstead.com/essays/david.html

Sardar, Z. *Orientalism*. Buckingham: Open University Press, 1999.

Saslow, James M. *The Poetry of Michelangelo: An Annotated Translation*. New York: Yale University Press, 1991.

Sayers, D. L., trans. *The Divine Comedy, Part 3: Paradise*. London: Penguin Classics, 1962.

Seguy, Marie-Rose. *The Miraculous Journey of Mahomet*. New York: George Braziller, 1977.

Sewell, B. 'Sinan: The Architect of a Forgotten Renaissance.' *Cornucopia*, 1992/93.

Shearman, John. *Mannerism*. London: Penguin Books, 1967.

Smith, T. *Turkish Sufi Poets: Lives and Poems*. Victoria, Australia: New Humanity Books, 2014.

Steinberg, L. 'Michelangelo's Last Judgement as Merciful Heresy.' *Art in America* 63 (1975): 53-63. Accessed August 11, 2016. https://www.artinamericamagazine.com/news-features/magazines/from-the-archives-michelangelos-last-judgement-as-merciful-heresy/

The Age of Süleyman the Magnificent. NSW, Australia: Art Exhibitions Australia / Beagle Press, 1990, Exhibition Publication.

Tolnay, C. de. *Michelangelo: The Final Period.* New York: Princeton University Press, 1960.

Tolnay, C. de. *Michelangelo: Sculptor, Painter, Architect. New* York: Princeton University, Press, 1975.

Trutty-Coohill, Patricia. 'Agathos in Michelangelo's Sistine Ceiling.' Accessed June 28, 2015. http://www.agathos-international review.-com/issue1/articles/01_AGATHOS_IN_MICHELANGELO_-SISTINE_CEILING.pdf

Tüfekçi, A. 'Books, syllabuses, ijazah: A look into the educational system in Ottoman madrassas,' *Daily Sabah* (December 2, 2020). Accessed December 11, 2020. https://www.dailysabah.com/arts/books-syllabuses-ijazah-a-look-into-the-educational-system-in-ottoman-madrassas/news

Vakfiye Genel Müdürlüğü (VGM). Defter 648.

Vasari, Giorgio. *Lives of the Painters, Sculptors and Architects.* Translated by Gaston du C. de Vere with an introduction and Notes by David Ekserdjian. London: Everyman's Library, 1996.

Vasari, G. *The Lives of the Painters, Sculptors and Architects.* Translated by Jonathan Foster. New York: Dover Publications, 2005. Kindle Edition.

Vasari, G. *The Lives of the Painters, Sculptors and Architects.* Edited by William Gaunt, 4 vols. New York: Dent, 1963.

Vasari, G. *Le vite de' piu eccellenti pittori, scultori ed architetti* (Torino: Letteratura italiana Einaudi, 1986. Accessed April 3, 2016. http://www.letteraturaitaliana.net/pdf/Volume_5/t129.pdf.

Vasari, G. Le vite de' piu eccellenti architetti pittori, et scultori italiani da Cimabue insino a'tempi nostril. Firenze: Torentino, 1550. Accessed April 3 2016. http://bepi1949.altervista.org/vasari/vasari10.htm

Vasari, G. *Part I of The Lives*. Accessed April 3, 2016. http://members.efn.org/~acd/vite/VasariGioPisano.htm1

Vasari, G. *Part III of The Lives*. Accessed May 5, 2016. http://members.efn.org/~acd/vite/VasariMichelangelo7.html

Wallace, William E. *Michelangelo: The Artist, the Man, and His Times*. New York: Cambridge University Press, 2010. Kindle Edition.

Willis, M. D. "Tiles from the Mosque of Rüstem Paşa in Istanbul". *Artibus Asiae*, Vol. 48, No. 3/4. Artibus Asiae Publishers, 1987.

Winter, Tim, ed. *The Cambridge companion to Classical Islamic Theology*. United Kingdom: Cambridge University Press, 2008.

Yerasimos, S. *Constantinople: Istanbul's Historical Heritage*. Paris: H. F. Ullmann Publishing, 2012.

Zweig, Connie, and Jeremiah Abrams, eds. *Meeting the Shadow: The Hidden Power of the Dark Side of Human Nature*. New York: Penguin Putnam Inc., 1991.

Ziai, H. *The Book of Radiance*. Tehran: Mazda Publisher, 1998.

www.ingramcontent.com/pod-product-compliance
Lightning Source LLC
Chambersburg PA
CBHW060848170526
45158CB00001B/281